# The Gospel of the Long Walk

# The Gospel of the Long Walk

Rev. Meddy Jacques

Rev. Jeffrey E. Jacques

***The Gospel of the Long Walk*** *is a work of fiction. Names, characters, places and incidents either are the product of the authors' imagination or are used fictitiously. Any resemblance to actual events, places or persons, living or dead, is entirely coincidental.*

*Copyright © 2012 by Rev. Meddy Jacques and Rev. Jeffrey E. Jacques. All rights reserved.*

ISBN: 978-0-9848242-2-9
First Edition

Publisher: Ushered Path Publishing

www.facebook.com/GospelOfTheLongWalk

*Cover and book design: Rev. Meddy Jacques & Rev. Jeffrey E. Jacques*

*Front cover art and illustrations are the original works of Nadia N. Thompson. Copyright © 2012. All rights reserved.*

*Back cover photography courtesy of Rev. Meddy Jacques & Rev. Jeffrey E. Jacques. Copyright © 2012. All rights reserved.*

To David, and the efforts of his Family,
*who made the path clear to the throne;*

To Nadia and Brenden,
*whom have suffered greatly the pains of these chapters;*

and

To Joanne and Pete,
and
To Helen and John.
*They gave us this beginning.*

Praise be to God!

*"If I speak with human eloquence
and angelic ecstasy
but don't love,
I'm nothing
but the creaking of a rusty gate.*

*If I speak God's Word with power,
revealing all his mysteries
and making everything plain as day,
and if I have faith that says to a mountain,
"Jump," and it jumps,
but I don't love,
I'm nothing.*

*If I give everything I own to the poor
and even go to the stake to be burned as a martyr,
but I don't love,
I've gotten nowhere.*

*So, no matter what I say,
what I believe,
and what I do,
I'm bankrupt without love."*

*~ 1 Corinthians 13:1-7*

# Notes from the Authors

Although this is a work of historical fiction based in the time of beloved biblical figures, we have our own understandings of events from those times. Many of the names, characters, places and incidents are a product of our own "imagination," and some will see it as pure fiction. Yet, it is the message behind the works of fiction that inspire lives to change. Are the dreams and memories in your own mind works of fiction, or are they more?

It saddens us that the life of a great man, with the radiant spark of divinity within, was edited and translated to the whim of those who wished to control society for their own ego and affluence. All He came to do in this incarnation was to share the knowledge of the ancients and of Love with all. Instead He received a death sentence because of his "blasphemous" life. A life filled with a desire to teach how to live within the Law from within the heart and soul – not because the Law demands it, but because it brings peace and serenity. It is our hope that you read these words feeling the love in your heart through the eyes of a different point of view from those who have been discounted throughout the centuries.

May the clouds be wiped away from the Light of Knowledge so that the Truth shines brightly. Our personal messages follow, yet from both of us...

May Peace and Love<br>reign in your hearts<br>forever more.

Growing up today is so different than even the toddling age of my now teenage children. For many years, we read books as a family at bedtime. Although the titles may have changed from my youth, the fairy tale adventures continued with witches and wizards with evolving personalities. In those stores, while those dressed in robes often abused their powers, there was always one who would rush in and save the day, often wearing the white. To live happily ever after, Good must triumph over evil.

One of the games I played as a child was called "telephone." One thought of a sentence and whispered it once into the ear of the child sitting next to them. This continued around the circle until the last person spoke out loud what they had heard. All would laugh at how even the simplest statement devolved into some extraordinary and often nonsensical phrase. Each child repeated from memory what was familiar to their ears. Through no fault of their own, each player further corrupted the text, the words changing ever so slightly with each utterance that perhaps only a word or two remained of the original.

So perhaps that is the origin of all fairy tales, even the modern ones. Think about how we use our words. Which one of us has not known a talking donkey? Not all things that are groovy have ridges and what I call hot, my children may find cool or even sick. However, I think we often agree on what is truly awesome.

So what is this story that some will hold, turning paper pages, and some will scroll through on a screen? Written from two points of view, some will say it is fiction, some will cry out blasphemy, while others will embrace a maligned character whose tears revealed the Truth. As for me, I call it a love story that will never end.

Blessings,

*Meddy*

While I agree with "she who walks with my braid in her hand," I still wonder how you will see yourself in this story, this lifetime of memory and of love. Will you cry out to the words before you as heathen blasphemy or truly feel the words within your soul, searching for the element of truth that rings deep within your heart? The story of a great man filled with Love for all beings, corrupted by the desires of Kings, becomes the clanging of a rusty gate I choose not to enter. Before you read these pages and the coming chapters of lives lived through all the depths of creation, emotion and chaos, remember that the underlying element of everything is Love. Every underlying element in your own life is Love or the desire to reclaim the Love you feel has been lost.

We may see many friends come from these words you are about to read; and many friends may go. Yet all come and go with our love and prayers on the winds that guide them through life. It is my hope that the message of the love story within them, the love between brothers, between a man and a woman, between parents and children, and for those who were not of his seed, will inspire you to Love all around you.

Allow the words of a man whom I know lost sight of the true meaning of that life for a time – until the Truth set him free – to guide you through our story we must tell you now.

*When you opened a door I shut long ago I loved you for that;*
> *because my soul had been resurrected*
> *from the embers of the fire that still exists*
> *deep in my Heart.*

*I have tried to quell that which hurts;*
    *which seems to rule my life.*
    *I envisioned an end to my curse.*
    *Yet you renewed my hopes and my fears*
    *of those days in which I had intended*
    *to forget.*
*How can you expect*
    *to show your soul – so beautiful, so eloquent.*
    *To be able to see that which lies so deep*
    *within you; and yet not be able*
    *to see that which you seek*
    *sits right in front of you?*
*Such rambling on is senseless.*
    *My heart is shown –*
    *open unto your slings and arrows.*
*Or, if your wish be*
    *to join me in this Journey,*
    *so let it be.*
    *I have seen your soul,*
    *and will forever be changed.*
*And my heart offered unto your mercy.*
    *My wish and hopes open to you.*
*Please let this one reach you.*

                                               Love to all of you,

# What You Haven't Been Told

# ~ Chapter 1 ~

# The Doubting Thomas

*"Then Jesus told him, "Because you have seen me, you have believed; blessed are those who have not seen and yet have believed." ~ John 20:29*

Yehuda, covered in dust, came finally into the upper room where the rest all had been waiting to hear from their Master, now arisen from the dead. Peter may have saved Yehuda, or something may have saved him, and now recovered, he had to tell them what had happened. The door had been pushed inward with such ferocity; many of those still remaining in the room believed that the time of reckoning had come early for them.

Yehuda's family, or once a family he called close to his heart, were all huddled around each other listening to a story being told by Miriam and Miryam who had waited at Yosef of Arimathea's tomb where Yeshua had been laid just prior to sunset, as the Law commanded.

While he knew something else had happened due to the exhilarated attention all were giving Miriam, his mother, Yehuda's mind could barely be drawn from the horror he had witnessed. The miracle of his being saved from his own designed demise was a miracle enough to recant to everyone gathered. The memory of the events of the last few days was still vivid in his mind.

"How dare you enter this holy place?" thundered Andrew as Yehuda advanced through the doorway. Yehuda stood there in such desperation, almost on the verge of mental destruction. He had desired to be the one to take the punishment from the Romans and the Sanhedrin, yet that was not in the plan. He had desired to follow Yeshua to the heavens, yet that was not in the plan. He had wished to be left alone, yet that was not in the plan. He believed that he might find some solace with his family here in the upper room in his uncle's home, yet that was not in the plan. Andrew rushed across the room with anger on his face and in his heart.

"Brother, enough! Andrew! You do not know nor understand the torment that his brother has been through! Leave him be!" Peter grabbed Andrew by the collar and held him to the wall.

Distress wrinkling his face, "What is it everyone is so enthralled about?" Yehuda asked to divert the attention that Andrew was creating.

It was Simon Peter who began to recant the story of the miracle of which Miriam and Miryam were witnesses. "He's alive, Yehuda! He has risen! As he had told all of us!"

"Seriously, Peter?" Yehuda could not, would not, believe the words from Peter. So much they had been through over the years, and still some measure of doubt occupied his mind. "He still lives?"

Turning his head in a directed understanding at Yehuda, "Would I, after the miracle we both witnessed not even a day ago, tell you a lie?" Yehuda acquiesced to an extent, yet drew his eyes from Peter. Peter contemplating his desire to be understood fully, strained to look into Yehuda's eyes again, "Would I, who caught you as you fell, deceive you?"

Yehuda had been drawn down by many emotions – doubt, fear, dismay and depression to name a few – yet doubt had returned and not mistrust as Peter had eluded. "It is neither deceit nor mistrust with which I charge you, Peter. It is doubt that clouds my understanding. I fear that until I hold him again, until I feel the wounds that still ache in my own wrists, until I wash his feet and press my thumbs into his wounds, I will not truly believe that what everyone heard has happened has truly come to pass. He is gone."

"Brother. Yehuda! Do not take on the anger and disappointment of that crowd into your heart. As the Master said, 'Hold neither regret nor guilt in your heart. Next to fear, guilt is the greatest hindrance to truly seeing the Light and the Way to the Lord,' and none of us should forget that. Most of all you should not forget, Yehuda, as his brother and twin. What he knew, you knew. John saw you writhe in pain alongside of him on the hill at the cross."

Looking down at his hands and feet as he sat by the door, he could still feel the pain, the broken bones that did not exist in his hands. He felt the blood pouring from the soles of his feet, yet no pool would serve as proof to sensations he was still suffering. "More to the point, I think I would prefer to see evidence of the pain and wounding I received, yet clean and fresh is my body."

Miriam heard the commotion that Andrew had made and rushed to her son's side. She grabbed his hand, picked him up from the floor onto his feet with such excitement not seen in some time, and leaned into him with all the love of a mother. She looked up at him softly yet glowing with love, "Yehuda, my son. It is true. He is gone from the tomb my brother laid him in."

Still caught in the emotion of losing his other half, and from being saved and released from his own tree, "Yes, Ima. I have seen it, too." Yehuda wanted to tell her that he had been down at the tomb. He had seen the soldiers frozen where they were. The world had changed so much in the last few days.

Miriam clung to Yehuda still as she told him of what his brother had revealed to her and Miryam. However, he had not heard a word she said, just simply held her as she would him when he was young and needed the embrace of his mother.

"Yehuda, my son, have you heard anything I have said?" Miriam still relaxed into his chest yet she knew that his attention was not in the moment, and definitely not on her words. "Yehuda," not gaining any response, she gently tapped the back of his head, grabbed his chin and looked into his eyes. "Yehuda, look at me. I know the pain you feel. When you two were or are in pain, so am I. Never will I forget him hanging on that tree, yet it will not be how I see him. I see him as I see you – my son."

Yehuda looked at his Ima and a tear fell from his eye, "Ima." He looked straight into her eyes.

He felt his Ima, and now it would be his turn to rest in his mother's arms. The everlasting and comforting arms that held him tightly and claimed him as her own, equal in every way to Yeshua.

"Ima?" Yehuda pleaded. Miriam simply held him tightly as they both slid down the wall, more under the weight of her son who could no longer stand.

Always in his Ima's eyes was Yehuda an equal to Yeshua. "Ima," was all he could muster amid the tears and sobbing that overcame his silent demeanor from the terrors he had encountered.

"Ima! Ima! Ima!" Yehuda began to say over and over, as Miriam rocked him gently and slowly. She began to hum a simple tune that would always calm his troubled heart as an infant. As she brushed his hair, she could see the faint marks of twisted rope, and she simply looked to the skies as if she were about to pray. Yet, nothing but tears came from Miriam. Soon his exclamations turned into silent weeping in the true light of a mother's love for her son.

She lowered her head, grabbed his chin once again to bring it to her eyes, "It is the truth I tell you, Yehuda. You are meant for great things too, my son. Many years ago, my heart was torn in two; and those two pieces of my heart were to be the saviors of this world. I knew then what the Angel of the Lord told me, and I still know it to this day. Nothing has changed, Yehuda. You are my heart. It pains me to see you in this state, yet there is only one person who can bring you from the darkness – and he will be here soon. He told us to come and tell everyone to wait for him here. You will see."

Yehuda, grasping at his chest, almost reached inward to pull out his beating heart, yet through the tears he looked into his Ima's eyes again. He pounded his chest and ripped his robe, "Ima, my heart."

"Yes, my son. I know. There is no need for Shiva."

"No, Ima. While I mourn not having him close to me, it is something else. My heart, Ima, it still beats."

Smiling to calm his nerves, "Of course it does, Yehuda, and I can feel your chest rise and fall also."

Yehuda became slightly more insistent with Miriam, "Ima, no! I mean that my heart still beats as it did when he was alive. It has been said by many holy men that Yeshua and I are of one heart. They say that 'one heart torn will not beat if one dies.' I felt my heart stop there on the hill beneath his torn body. Only for a moment that seemed a lifetime, yet it began again when the light went away, and it beats still!" He placed his Ima's hand on his heart, and it beat strongly as it always had.

Miriam began to panic at the possibility of madness setting into her son's mind. "Why, yes Yehuda. It beats strong!" A look of concern for his well-being crossed over her face, masked by a weary smile.

Yehuda could read her concern, "Oh, Ima, do not worry. I have not lost the sense of life. Even Yeshua, in my darkest of days, came to me when I called him and he told me, 'Heart of my heart. I will not let you go, for in doing so I must also go. Where you go, I will go. If you stay, I will stay. As long as our hearts beat, the Light will not diminish. If one of us goes, so must the other.' So I know he is still alive!"

Matching his excitement, "Yes, indeed my son! He is very much alive! He has been taken into the heavens for a renewed life with a greater mission. He will be coming back upon the wings of the holiest of holies. Their majesty and abilities are great. They fly like angels on the winds, yet they held no wings on their backs."

Her gaze fell to confusion, yet quickly back to radiant triumph as she recalled what she and Miryam had witnessed. "He told us that he will return to us on great light, and that you, Miryam and the children could not be seen by anyone outside of this mixed family. Please believe me, Yehuda. Yeshua will return to us!"

"Until I see the wounds for myself, I will remain." With that, Yehuda slowly made his way to the window facing the eastern skies. He looked longingly, waiting for a sign in the heavens for his brother's return. Miriam quietly whimpered by the doorway from where Yehuda had retired to the windows. "My Yehuda, my Yehuda. You are my heart, Yehuda. My Yehuda."

# ~ Chapter 2 ~

# Nailed to a Tree

*"The metalworker encourages the goldsmith, and the one who smooths with the hammer spurs on the one who strikes the anvil. One says of the welding, 'It is good.' The other nails down the idol so it will not topple." ~ Isaiah 41:7*

Yehuda had witnessed the horror of his brother being nailed to the planks of what was once a sacred tree. Each strike of the hammer as it pierced further and further into Yeshua's flesh tore a part of him at the same time. The blood and fluids that flowed from his skin stuck like sap to the cross. Each droplet of blood that stained the ground of Golgotha resounded in his ears as if the Lord struck each grain with lightning.

When he thought he could bear not one more sound, the centurions moved to the next wrist and it all began again. Strike one, and Yehuda's wrist wrought in agony as the dull pointed spike pierced the roughened fabric of his skin, tearing at it and digging through the layers of flesh. Time slowed as he yearned for it to speed up so that this pain could be lessened, yet there was a reason. With the second strike of the hammer, he could feel the dullest sharpness of the spike rip through his wrist; the burning torture, paralyzing him while his entire being writhed with each numbing blow. Strike three, as the tip of the spike ripped the tendons of his brother's wrist and pierced through the back of his arm into the wood, Yehuda yearned for release weeping upon the rocks at his feet.

The pain was so excruciating, his ears began to ring with misery, drowning out the wailing of his Ima and the rest of the women gathered to witness this atrocity. Just as his mind could take no more, his head lilted to the right and his tear and pain-stained vision looked upon Yeshua crying out in agony without sound. As their eyes met, both fell silent and merely smiled.

The demonic laughter of the soldiers that delighted in the barbaric treatment taking place was halted while one of them barked orders to place a block below Yeshua for "his majesty to rest his feet." That brief moment was torn from their union of mind, soul and love as Yehuda dropped to his side when Yeshua's back arched high as the last spike pierced the top foot. The centurions had placed one foot over the other, and struck with more might knowing this last spike had to make it through both feet and the plank of the cross.

Yehuda collapsed onto his back in almost a mirrored fashion to his brother's posture. Some of the guards laughed at Yehuda's pain, tossing and kicking rocks at him. He noticed none of their stoning as all he felt was each agonizing blow after blow, each stinging jolt to each and every bone, ligament and sinew. The pain brought Yehuda to the point of exhaustion where he thought he might lose consciousness. Each time, however, his gaze would fall on Yeshua, and the peace between them would reign in the torment they both could feel.

As the cross was lifted, a sense of relief from the piercing blows he had empathically felt was masked as his eyes met Yeshua's. Everyone that had gathered was struck in a moment of silence as the cross fell into the hole that held it upright. There hung his brother, the savior from the darkness that followed him all his life. Memories of Yeshua laying in the garden when they were young, crying and wailing in some angelic ecstasy, sometimes in pain mixed with pure joy, was all that crept into Yehuda's mind. Could Yeshua have seen this all those years ago? He had remained so calm since they entered Jerusalem.

He remembered a discussion not too long ago, "You will not always have me." Could he have truly known? How could he have known?

Yehuda began to pray, praying harder than he had ever prayed before. He was a devout man in his faith, even though he had waivered in practice from time to time. As he prayed, time seemed to drag on longer than it would normally. Memories of their times together – the happy times with Yeshua, the laughter, talks and hours spent in silence marveling at the majesty of creation all around them – played through Yehuda's mind to temper the pain and emotions that were raging through his physical body.

With the remaining sensations of the ordeal that had only just begun, Yehuda made his way to Miryam, and held close to her. He shrieked in his anguish, "It should have been me!" As Yehuda slumped down away from his mother and his brother's wife, he repeated much more subdued, "It should have been me!"

He could hold his strength no longer as waves of guilt and sadness, remorse and folly, despair and madness, all the frailty of humanity came rushing over him like breakers on the shores. Already on his knees, he buckled forward and sobbed beside Miryam. His

Ima's hands stroked the back of his head to try and soothe her son's pain. She herself searched for a savior to release her from the suffering she witnessed in both of her sons.

Through the tears he heard the strained voice of Yeshua speaking down to Miryam, "Woman." Both Miriam and Miryam looked up to his lashed and bruised face, stained with shades of crimson blood. Miriam gently and lovingly switched her gaze to Miryam, the only other woman who could feel as helpless as she did, yet such love still poured from her face; it brought both of them to more tears. Either in paralytic pain or by desired direction, Yeshua looked upon the sobbing heap of his brother. Yehuda was exasperated with the floods of emotions falling on him. "Look upon your husband." Her eyes locked on Yeshua, Miryam slowly turned to place a hand on Yehuda.

According to the Law, no woman without children was to be abandoned upon the death of her husband. Either by design or default through the right of redemption, the marriage contract passed to the next unmarried brother of age. In this concluding act, Yeshua challenged the tradition of yibbum, as he had confronted those about to stone the adulteress, but he would not leave either to mourn alone. The past would now be left where it was meant to be – unchangeable and serving as a place to begin anew – in the past.

A rush of peace fell on Yehuda, and he beheld his brother. The stains of blood, the lacerations of the skin, the ravaged visage of his brother hanging on the tree – all of these began to fade and renew themselves in Yehuda's eyes. Yeshua was glowing with all the colors of creation from a light that streamed from the gathering clouds. Time stopped for the four of them. He looked up to Yeshua, tears streaming from his face and pooling on the ground beneath him. He strained in desire to touch him, yet only his head and neck could strive to rise beneath the pain ravaging his body as well. "Brother."

The hand of his Ima on the center of his back, pouring all the tenderness she could into him for both he and Yeshua. She could not touch her hanging son, yet she knew he could feel her love through his twin. The hand of Miryam, resting gently on the back of his neck, knowing the pain Yehuda was going through, held him so that he could see and hear his brother.

"Brother, look upon your wife." The charge placed upon him was the only choice Yeshua could make for his dying will to bypass the Law. With those last words, Yehuda arose to sit on his heels, Miryam holding close to him; his Ima, placing her head on his shoulder. They all looked up to their beloved son, brother and husband. Tears flowed down their faces as the skies drew dark. The winds began to gale sending fear through every soldier as they were casting lots to own a piece of this man they had harassed for hours. Terror was wrought on the guilty gathered, and many fled this now sanctified ground.

A colossal cloud hovered as an immense tower that mushroomed above this mount, and from it a beam of light parted the darkening mass. As the beam rained down, Yeshua combed the vast swirling expanse of clouds carrying the angels of impending doom. Searching the skies for the source of their light, he called out to them and implored for all to hear as the voice of the sacrificial lamb, "Elohim, Elohim, do not forsake them!"

The vibrations in the air created a sound few men had ever heard before. Yeshua cried out again, "Abba, forgive them. They know not what they do." The air became thick and tense.

Through the pain ravaging his body to the point of numbing acceptance of the physical release that was taking place, Yeshua lilted to his left. He declared to the thief that had, in his final moments of life, truly understood all that had transpired and all that was about to happen, "Truly, friend, you will be with me this day in paradise."

At this instant, the clouds glowed as if containing the sun itself. Yeshua arched his back, straining to look to the heavens at a great light forming to a point directly above his head, "Father... Into your hands I commend my spirit." At those words, the humming quickened and the air became lighter and lighter with each reverberation of sounds from the heavens.

Whether through exhaustion or desire for this ordeal to be over, Yeshua looked to Miriam and a tear fell from his eye. He longed for his mother's embrace one last time. "I thirst."

From all around them came this gale force wind. On that gust carried the voices of a host of otherworldly beings, clamoring unknown tongues. What could have been hours of time seemed to compress into a rush of seconds. Suddenly with a hush, Yeshua proclaimed, "It is done."

The ground shook as it never had before as if it were about to open wide and swallow all into the belly of the Earth. Cries from the city could be heard; cries of fear and reprisal for the acts that had taken place.

The light that had been encompassing Yeshua shrunk back into the clouds with the sound of a great bellows drawing in a tempest. As the light receded, many of those, including Yehuda, Miriam and Miryam, were drawn up to their feet with great ease. It was almost as if the force that held all solid on the ground had been lessened. Pebbles rose off the ground, the blood encrusted hair on Yeshua began to lift and float. His once drooping body had almost seemed to stand, nailed to that cross.

A deafening silence came upon the hill, the shrill vacuum painfully flooding their ears. After a sudden inrush of breath, Yeshua's lips let loose his spirit. Voices from every direction in the heavens, as when Miriam gave birth to him, heralded his apparent death. All in creation knew he had been released. The pain and agony that was visibly evident across every inch of his body, was now gone.

The lifeless body of his brother fell limp and Yehuda's gaze fell onto Yeshua's darkened eyes. Realizing that his heart too had stopped, Yehuda was astonished that his pain was gone for a brief moment. The nothingness he felt inside him was too hard to bear. The voices were silent, pain had no foothold and the unending persecution from the shadows was felt no more. Was this death? The sudden thump within his chest answered a resounding, "Not yet, brother."

He stopped and looked to the skies that he hoped would bring his release as well. He had felt his heart break at those last words his brother uttered, yet something was still the same as it had been. His heart was still whole?

He rose to his feet, touched the hair of his Ima, and placed a hand on her shoulder and one on Miryam's. "This cannot be. I cannot be without him. I love you all." They had not heard a word.

Yehuda began a slow exit from the base of the cross, clutching at his chest. Yeshua was gone. Yehuda's reason for being was gone. All they talked about, all they planned now changed. Everything had changed. Yehuda's head lifted slowly to the horizon, and even though the tears had dried up and he felt no more could fall, one single tear tumbled from his eye. It rolled down his cheek and struck the ground with the sound of great lightning.

The ground shook again, and from his face withdrew all color, all emotion. He stood arms and hands limp at his side. Yehuda looked up to the skies, "Abba Elohim, it is truly done. I am coming home."

# ~ Chapter 3 ~

# To the Garden

*"You must not leave the body hanging on the pole overnight. Be sure to bury it that same day, because anyone who is hung on a pole is under God's curse. You must not desecrate the land the LORD your God is giving you as an inheritance." ~ Deuteronomy 21:23*

"Wherever you go, I will go. Where you stay, I will also stay. The gifts our Father in Heaven left us, brother, will keep you well throughout your days. Yehuda, you must do what we came here to do." Gifts sometimes feel as a curse, and burn like the tears that fell from Yehuda's chin that ghastly night. The last thing he whispered to Yeshua as they embraced, "You must do what we came here to do." Not all of his brothers in flesh or spirit heard what was said, and the looks in their eyes would sear his heart for many generations to come.

Peter could muster an army of men, yet nothing could have stopped Yehuda from fleeing that place. Peter cried out to Yehuda as he turned and ran, "Yehuda! Yehuda!"

The winds carried Yehuda faster and faster past the city. Peter should have returned to Miriam and everyone at Golgotha and the horror that Yehuda could no longer stomach. He needed to leave everything behind, no matter what plan had been agreed. Yehuda ran so quickly in the madness of grief that exhaustion came to his legs quickly. Yehuda tumbled underneath the pressure, falling to his knees, and in turn careening down the hillside.  The descent from crest of the hill should have killed him, yet the rotting corpse of some beast of burden broke his fall.  When he opened his eyes, the tears stinging the newly formed scratches on his face, all he could see through the haze was the white fur and the harsh hum of flies; the sound rang through his ears like a swarm of invading soldiers.  Could that rotting beast been the same colt Yeshua rode into Jerusalem as the King he deserved to be?  How fitting that the rope used to bridle his royal carriage would finally put Yehuda to rest – or so he thought.  Peter was much slower than Yehuda and if the storm of emotions had not carried him past Peter's ability to catch up to him, the fall from the path would surely elude his chase.

Peter bellowed, "Yehuda!  Yehuda!  Get down from there!"

Yehuda muttered under his breath, "Too late, my friend.  I go to be with my brother."

Whether it was the crack of the dead branch above him, or the hefty thud in Peter's arms that saved his contrived fate, Yehuda was once again redeemed.  Kept once again from the lot he egotistically designed for himself!  Who was he to design the fate of anyone or anything?  Had he not learned from being saved in that alley all those years ago?

In Yehuda's mind, he heard, "The gifts our Father in Heaven left to us, brother, will keep us safe.  Yehuda, you must do what we came here to do."  Yehuda cried up to Peter through his eyes, "If I had not seen the nails pierce his skin.  If only the shudder of his last breath had not ushered the gale that followed and announced his demise, I would have thought Yeshua had caught me."

Those bulky arms and burly chest were the only understanding that it was truly Peter who held Yehuda and stopped him. Or was it Peter? The hand on his scar had no callouses and reached further than Peter's could have. Yeshua would always find a way to save his brother from himself. Feeling the air constricted by the rope still hanging from his neck, Yehuda looked up at Peter and forced two simple words, "Bless you."

# ~ Chapter 4 ~

# The Upper Room

*"He will show you a large upper room, all furnished. Make preparations there." ~ Luke 22:12*

In the upper room of his Uncle's house, more than fourscore were assembled who had been touched by the Light emanating from the heavens, and had seen Yeshua taken up into the sky. Among them were his closest friends and disciples: Lazareth and his wife, Martha; Simon (that Yeshua had named Peter), with his brother Andrew; and the Boanerges, James and John; along with the lifelong companions Philip and Bartholomew; the oldest brothers: Joses with his family, Matthew, the prodigal son, and Simon the Zealot along with their mother Miriam and husband Yosef, the elder, who being the senior was also called Cleopas, but known as Alpheus to the Greeks, and Yosef's brother Zebedee with his wife; his youngest brothers and some of his sisters and their families, his wife Miryam and their children Tzmech, Sarah, Elisheva, Migdala, Uzit, Halva and little Maimon, and of course, his twin, Yehuda, to whom he had left his heart. Yosef came in with those from the lower apartments of the house on the hill called Maath and was accompanied by his wife and their children and their children. His hood still drawn, Nicodemus was the last to enter the room. With a nod from Simon Peter, Yosef brought out from around his neck the key and locking the door, sat to comfort his sister, Miriam.

Simon Peter, at the nod from the two Pharisees loyal to this gathering, led them in prayer and recited from the Psalms. "In the morning, from us will Yehuda depart, leaving our numbers lacking. Who will be raised up as a witness? Who will risk his flesh to testify yet against the Sanhedrin in the name of Yeshua and all that is Truth?"

At that time, Barabbas stood as did Matthias. Simon Peter nodded and then lifted his arms in prayer, "Lord, you know everyone's heart. Show us which of these men you would choose to continue your ministry as Yehuda leaves us to go where you chose for him."

At that moment, a sound like a mighty storm came from the heavens, although no wind stirred at the windows. Even in the streets, crowds gathered in bewilderment at the sound and the rays of multicolored light that beamed down upon them. Each beam that washed over them radiated out luminous colors and as it spiraled over them, their hearts filled with song and they knew the need of their neighbor. In addition, those in the upper rooms were flooded with the sound of bells as each was given the wisdom of the languages of men. And there, in their midst, stood Yeshua, who laid his hand on the shoulder of Barabbas. Barabbas fell to his knees. "I will witness to all the glory I have seen, my Lord and my Savior."

Yeshua smiled at Barabbas, "You, with neither a father nor mother to claim you, were raised amongst thieves; your life has been a testament of what one can do in the name of justice for our people. From this day shall you be known always and only as Justus, who fought with honor against our oppressors. It was the will and the desire of the people, Justus, which has saved you. Even your will is greater than that which my hand may save."

Yeshua continued after a brief pause and stepped toward Matthias, "Yet for the purposes of witnessing, you, Matthias, do I choose. The days of Barabbas have been long in the wrestling with the Romans. Your fresh face will travel much further and with less scrapes."

Matthias gave a simple nod, but his knees overcome with joy, like one drunk with wine, then sunk to the floor.

Yeshua turned back to Barabbas, "It is my desire that you remain the companion to my Mother and to Yosef and to those who need your sword and your eyes." Yeshua placed his hands upon the older man's head, his crumpled face and the blighted eye from the taunts of the centurions returned to its former, handsome countenance of youth. His beard grew out where it had been shaved off in the Roman fashion when he was arrested, a punishment of shame by the Sadducees. None who would behold him now would know his former name. "Justus, is it your will to do this?"

Barabbas stood and embraced him. Those who would see could see him float from the floor in his bliss. "My Lord and my redeemer, as you will it, it is done." And Barabbas went and sat at the feet of their host and Miriam, for whom he had forsaken any marriage because of his love for her.

Yeshua went and stood before Simon, "Peter, be the witness among all gathered here so that no man or woman or child is left without hope. Share the love that a father has for his child to lead our people back home. Cleave to your wife and be good to her and teach her what you have witnessed so that for all your generations, the light will shine. For a man who walks alone, is truly alone. At the end of the age, stand with those who have awakened. And when it is asked of you to answer to the name I have given you, do not deny me, for it will be then that you will know my return draws near."

Yeshua went and touched the heads and hands of those who were gathered and all did reach and touched his robes as he did pass. To some, like his brothers and sisters, he would speak and to some he would whisper to their ear, especially to their children who would clap their hands and laugh and smile. Without words, Yeshua embraced Nicodemus, reminding him that he was without blame. To Lazareth and Martha, the couple whom had housed his wife and children so often while he traveled, he was also silent, merely taking both their hands and holding them against his chest as he peered into their eyes with an outpouring of love. And then he made his way to Yosef, their host, and gave him thanks for the risk and the sacrifices he had made after the crucifixion. Next was to Cleopas, who claimed him always as his own, and to Miriam, his mother, whose tears had only stopped flowing because the well had been emptied. He kissed her but said no more for their goodbyes had been made weeks before.

And to Yehuda, he embraced and immediately Yehuda wailed and sobbed in his arms. For all to hear, Yeshua stated, "Brother, all that came to the first is now come to you, the last but not the least. Brother, only you know all that my eyes have seen, but do not let these secrets pass with you. For even as your flesh shall perish, the knowledge of our father and of our home in the heavens should not perish. Teach my sons and my daughters to read and to pray and to be Kings and Queens of the ages to come." And then Yeshua brought his cheek against his brother's scar and felt all the pain and all the anger that still resided in the puckered folds that fed the reflection of his own gentle face; all the responsibility and blame that Yehuda felt, as if the circumstances were his to change. This test of humanity had failed, yet Yeshua, in his last act of compassion, to save them from the fate of the uncharitable Sodom and Gomorrah, had pleaded to the Elohim, "Do not forsake them!" Therefore, the storm from the heavens, which could have rent every stone into the sea, instead, merely tore asunder the veil.

Yeshua turned to all who had assembled in this upper room of the house in Arimathea. "My brothers and my sisters, I love you all. Although my spirit must leave you for a time, call upon me and my fathers in your time of need and in thanksgiving. Therefore, even as we may be far away, we shall hear your petitions and lend our strength."

"I send you out to all nations so that all may know my word is true so that my seed shall flourish wherever it is planted. From age to age, prepare for my homecoming. Find each other in your comings and your goings, for when you have all assembled, it will be then that I may return. Always, Elijah will be the trumpet to open up the path of my homecoming. Listen for his call in the night. Circle around his light."

"Do not grieve that I must leave you, for know that I go to prepare a place for you. Each of you will have a place in the heavens, brimming with milk and honey. Sleep now for I must depart."

With those words, the familiar slowing of time, the stillness and the quiet flooded Miryam's senses. All she could see was Him.

## ~ Chapter 5 ~

# The Division Multiplied

*"Only be careful, and watch yourselves closely so that you do not forget the things your eyes have seen or let them fade from your heart as long as you live. Teach them to your children and to their children after them." ~ Deuteronomy 4:9*

As Miryam continued to fold and refold her bedroll, Yeshua appeared beside her and placed that same hand we all knew on her head, and stroked her rumpled mane. "My dear, I must speak with my brother." The only answer was a demure smile from behind the waving auburn forest of her hair. "I'll attend to the children first and then let me speak with him for a bit before we have our time.... The children seem to be nearing the end of their day. Bring them here so I can have my whole family near me before I leave. Brother, will you join us?"

"Of course." His will be done, it was now his duty.

"Children," as Yeshua looked into the eyes of each of them, especially Miamon, yet none more than another, he held all at attention for what seemed an eternity. Such love poured from those amber eyes and that glow seemed to transfer out to the spellbound congregation of his family. Serenely comforting to Yeshua, he recalled how Yosef and Miriam, with their strong parental hands, had softly held both he and Yehuda so many times before. This time, he was not the child, but the father responsible to convey the strength in the gentleness of that touch.

"It is time for me to go on a long trip. Remember how we speak of the promised land of our people? Well, that's where I need to go. Your Uncle here loves you," his hand resting on Yehuda's left knee, "and he loves your mother, a great deal. Will you listen to him?" He followed their hesitant gaze as it slowly rested on Yehuda, especially from the older ones. Yeshua looked back at them, and continued, "If I say you should?"

Miamon held onto Yeshua's leg as if they were in the midst of a great storm. Maybe Yehuda's hand could one day calm the boy's mind like that blessed embrace to which he was accustomed. The rest looked at their father with such sadness, yet they always listened and heard his words. They barely needed to speak, and most refrained. Miamon just clung to his side. "Very good, little ones, go now and sleep. Your mother will attend to your bedsides and maybe you will dream of me and the places I must go. Know that your father loves you a great deal."

His voice breaking, "Our children, Miryam, tend to them, please. I will be with you soon. Fear not." Yehuda knew, looking at Miryam, that those green eyes would lose their brightness as soon as Yeshua departed for the last time. The gentle turn of his head toward where Yehuda sat near the slumbering Yosef and Miriam seemed almost theatrical. At the gesture, Yehuda stood. The angels would be playing the sweetest sounds if we could hear them.

Yeshua questioningly looked toward the light from above him, and it faded as they walked to the window alone. "Brother. My mirror, my friend, my torment, and yet, still my peace. I need you to do one last thing for me."

"It's always one last thing. Yet, all we've been through, this one more thing will be my pleasure. They are my own just as they are yours. Being an equal part of me, what is yours I will cherish as mine - for now and always."

"I feel your words are sincere, yet this one last thing will be a long walk for you. I cannot and will not be able to be a part of your physical life to come. I know how much you care for walking."

Unable to suppress the grin, Yehuda ignored the taunt. "We all knew that when you changed the plan. I may have disapproved of that choice, yet it was His will," glancing at the heavens in what could have been seen as a well-rehearsed sign of respect to our Creator, "and that's all that needs to be known."

"Brother, my face is well known, and will be known in the hearts and minds of many you will be meeting in your long years to come. My children and my wife need someone to keep their lives as I would - in safety of mind, heart and spirit. They will need a strong hand in the coming years."

"Whatever it is you need of me, it is your will and mine." Long-windedness was one of Yeshua's gifts, even now in the release of death.

"Carry them across the seas to a land where she will find peace. The walk will be long and the travel one of many trials." The scenes of distant shores flooded through Yehuda's mind with a dizzying speed that could have brought him to his knees if Yeshua hadn't had his arm securely around his shoulders. It was almost as if he could envision all the places and peoples they would be experiencing and meeting, preparing him for the years before their eyes.

Assimilating all that had been given to him with a sigh, Yehuda tried to reassure Yeshua who already knew the path before him. "They are your family and my family alike. They will be my family as long as you are separated from them."

"Know of the charge you take, dearest brother! It will be many generations before I return." Yehuda knew it, yet simply suppressed the understanding.

"They will always be yours, and I will keep them under my wing no matter what the barrier. Until you return, heart of my heart and mind of my mind," the tears choking his ability to speak, "and now family of my own. When you return, if they so choose at that time, they will be yours again." Turning to see the strength of that gaze which he had not seen in many years, he sat back on the deep sill of the window.

The moonlight broke through the clouds and illumined the words about to be returned to him, "Know this, Yeshua. Even before we broke the veil of this existence, what was to be yours was to be mine. We rebelled against that knowing many times, yet we knew it to be absolute. Enough, now brother, you must go and do what you must do. Her anxious ways are making me nauseous. Go to her as we will always have this connection. We always have. Find me if you need. Know always, I love you."

Appreciating Yehuda would hear the words in his thoughts, Yeshua responded, "Indeed, brother. More than you know, but will one day." A gentle grasp of the back of Yehuda's head as he pressed their brows together, the tears spilled from both their eyes. Enough flowed from both of them to fill a cup. "Know now that everywhere you go, you take me with you. We began as one being, we were brought into this world as two, and now I leave this world with you in it. I will no longer be by your side to remind you of the true path. Many will be there to guide you through this ever changing world, yet know that I will always... I will always be there if you call for me."

They both embraced for what seemed like a lifetime. When they finally drew away, their eyes caught one of the children's glances from across the room. Yeshua broke the silence, "Their eyes may flare and their words and actions may curse you, yet their hearts are the ones that yearn for something they can no longer have. That, my brother, causes me so much pain." Yeshua turned to block the glowers of daggers coming from Miryam. "I do not wish to cause you such pain. It's our face that they curse. It's the lack of my presence of which they are disappointed. It's her inability to touch my face, and the reminder of that scar I could not heal, that may cause you more pain that not even I or our Father can calm."

With a touch of his old self, with a smile, Yehuda growled, "Go now, before I leave them to another's care. Perhaps a Roman would do?" Even in the most somber of times, humor would make an appearance – sometimes appropriately and sometimes quite gracelessly. The silent gawp from his glowing eyes, even as the air turned awkward, still brought peace to Yehuda's mind. This time, he didn't mind the stare.

Yeshua's attention was drawn across his shoulder and behind him to Miryam and the children. Turning back to Yehuda with the comprehension that the inevitable was drawing close, "I am with you, always. I can choose no one better than my other self to lead them. I can choose no one better with whom to leave the treasure of my earthly kingdom. May all the solace you need be found in the grace and serenity of our Father. The road will be long, and I will return to embrace you once again at the doorstep of the new age. You need your rest."

"Do not tell me to sleep! I will rest when I feel..." Good and ready is often an entitlement best left to those who understand it more than the receiver, and now the unconscious state he fought drew closer. Yehuda would remember those eyes and that face for all of eternity. There was so much preparation, yet obviously not so much that a short respite couldn't postpone.

He may remember the face, the name, their lives and his grace and his mercy. The others will always remember Yehuda's name, and in many it will burn a hole in their minds and in the children's hearts for many years and generations to come. The memory of Yeshua would be all he needed to remind him of the truth. When it came time to unseal it, it would come back. Would they listen? Would they hear?

Will you listen? Will you hear?

## ~ Chapter 6 ~

## Sweetest Goodbyes

*"Mary Magdalene came and told the disciples that she
had seen the Lord, and that he had said
these things to her."
~ John 20:18*

"My beloved, blessed are you among women. Because of this, how greatly you will suffer. From age to age, they will persecute you because you know me, because I shall always be in your heart, and in your mind.

"My beloved, because of you, my cup was the most difficult to drink. But it is my father's will because of you also, that I must return to the heavens and make haste so that all who would see, and all that would hear, may find a new home amongst my family in the heavens.

"Take heart, my beloved, that I will come at the end of the age before all that you love has withered and I will carry you up to the home I prepare for you. Know this that I tell you is the truth from age to age. I will lead you in the righteousness and you will remain wise among women even though my wisdom also causes your flesh to perish. Fear not.

"The armies of man will follow you and you will be triumphant in my name. Fear not the reprisals of jealous men who will never hear my voice nor recognize my countenance though I shout and wave my many arms as I stand among them.

"Beloved, recognize your children from age to age. Recognize your brother and my brothers. Recognize from age to age those whom I have loved. Recognize my sisters as they will recognize you at the end of the age, though they may not understand this. Most of all, I give you the vision to see our daughters and our sons in the generations of those to come. They will perish in the flesh yet return near the end of the age. They will be greater than I in the line of David as Kings and be as powerful as the lionesses as Queens.

"In the end, my beloved, all will be filled with the essence of humility and courage. They will read the histories and know that each was given hope, yet the weak may triumph. Each will have their regents and each will have an understanding that the victories were short. None of it will matter at the end. Gather our family from the four winds when the signs show that I may be near once more.

"My beloved, look to Yehuda to keep you. Go from here and cross the sea. Yehuda will find safe passage with the banner of this house. Let none here know your landing for Rome would yet destroy a line of potential Kings, and the Sadducees and most of the Pharisees would only be glad to assist in keeping with the Caesars. Yehuda is now your husband by contract of the Law. Teach him what I could not, my beloved. Temper his lust for might and power. Temper his anger and wants. Keep him from hoarding for himself what could be used by others. He does not often see his own folly. Though our mother claimed us and Yosef presented us, he knows that others see him as no more than the rubbish of Sheol. Somehow those brief moments robbed him of the joy of life. Ah, the difference in those moments!

"Teach him what I have known – that the first shall be the last. He that serves comes to the Kingdom with greater portion. He that takes first and flouts it before the others will find an eternity waiting to be fed again. All our boyhood, our mother raised us up under the Law and under her love. Yehuda acted always as an only born so I know his path will continue this way for generations to see the difference. Be patient, my beloved, for it will be most difficult to keep his mind and heart on prospering others before himself. He will protect you with his blood and sinew, yet envy you also for his toil and his trial. Curse him not but love him more for the curse that befell him in those moments of coming late. One day he will understand the cup I have swallowed and bless his days. His generations will be many yet I shall have but this one to remember onward until the end of the age.

"My beloved, this will be the last moment of our embrace. As the sun rises, I will journey to the outer heavens. When I do return, I will find you then just as I have now. May the roses still bloom in your cheeks and the balsam anoint your feet.

"Sleep, my beloved. When the morning comes, each of us must travel far." Yeshua placed his forehead to hers. Miryam touched the silkiness of his hair and the curve of his jaw. She closed her eyes as the tears flooded her cheeks. He took both her hands in his and kissed her fingers.

"Will I see you again?" she whispered. Miryam pulled back to examine his face, his eyes and his hands so all would be marked in her memory.

"Yes. In all your dreams, I will be there when you think upon me. You will see me first when I come again. This I promise. Now sleep!" he gently chided with a smile that touched his eyes.

Yeshua walked Miryam through the aisles of those already snoring, stopping at her pallet. When she had assembled herself under the blanket, he bent and they shared a long, chaste kiss. "Sleep," he said. And she did.

# ~ Chapter 7 ~

# The Coming Dawn

*"Watchman, what of the night? The watchman said, The morning cometh, and also the night."*
*~ Isaiah 21:11-12.*

She woke without alarm to the stirrings near her. The children were quietly being roused to roll their blankets and make their travel packs. The stars were just beginning to fade. Yehuda looked her way as she sat up. He had been awake for what seemed hours, waiting for the sun to rise and knew that the cock who crowed ushered in a very long walk ahead of them. As their eyes met, she smiled gently but still he looked away from her.

Yehuda hurried the children in a light meal while Uncle Yosef directed the kitchens in preparing baskets for the journey. When all were fed and the sun pinked the sky, they set out with their cloaks and their sacks and their baskets and walked with the carts that Yosef had set aside for their Journey.

They reached the shore without delay. No one even looked upon them or questioned their movement, still astonished by the last evening's singing from the heavens. The words of Isaiah echoed in Miryam's ears as the Sovereign Lord spoke to those who would not understand like she did now, nor would in the last age.

Yehuda arranged all in the boats, the eldest with the youngest, each in order as the middle one took his hand. Simon Peter met them at the shore. He embraced

Yehuda with tears. "This task set upon me should be yours and I should carry this burden," with a gesture to Miryam and the children.

"Alas, let it be said," Yehuda challenged, "that though Cain slew Abel, it was my will to be my brother's keeper. What cup was his to drink must not poison the well. No burden will be heavier than this cup I hold but must not drink. Lest we rise up with him, let his Will be fulfilled."

Simon Peter shook his head in agreement. "He knew I would deny him thrice to only save my life. Let my life now save his memory forever."

Yehuda clapped his hand upon Peter's shoulder and remarked sadly, "May we return as friends at the end of the age." With all the disputes between them and the bitterness that had been on both their tongues, Simon Peter clasped the back of Yehuda's head and kissed him on his brow. "Yes, brother, may it be so."

Yehuda stepped into the boat, leaving Miryam and Simon Peter on the shore. Taking pause, Miryam reached for Peter's hand. "Peter," she said, using the name Yeshua had given him, "it has been long since you have been home to your wife and your family. Go home to them, Peter, as He did command. Make peace with them for your mission will require from them their love to carry you in the darkest hours. Without love, Peter, his words will be hollow gongs. All that you must do, it is because of his love for us that, yes, strengthens our resolve. Go home, Peter, and gather the strength for their hearts also. Teach what Yeshua showed you as well as what he spoke. Let no man of means or of law be separated from your table, nor be separate from the women. Most of all, remember that our children hold the spark of the fires that the Pharisees and the Sadducees sought to quench. Yea, though they will be washed away, others will take their stand. Do not give up the resolve to love them anyway. For surely as the cock crowed at your denial of his acquaintance, surely it was his love that has kept you free. Go home, Peter. Then shout from the mountaintops, as your path will be as footholds in the rock. Go now in peace, Peter, to love and serve all who would hear and all that would see."

Peter lifted her hand to his brow and fell to his knees. "Please, forgive me," he cried as he knelt before her. The years of pettiness and of jealousy weighed heavily on his back. Miryam had long suffered quietly the sting of his words and the daggers in his eyes. But his were no worse than the others. She saw that even Yehuda waited for her reply.

Pulling her hand from his, Peter fell forward. Miryam took his beard and lifted his face, "Rise up, Peter. For long have I drank from the cup poured out for my brother and for me from my birth. I danced with joy in the dust at my betrothal while my brother found peace in the scrolls and in the harshness of solitude. Yet with joy I watched him bathe the high and the low in the Jordan although most never understood why he did what he was called to do. While I bore children and delighted in their songs, my brother's head was cleaved from his body simply because his word was enough to undo Kings and raise the people in one voice. And my husband, my husband who could not be the victor of our people by tossing out the Romans! His love was greater to take the cross himself than see us all be hailed asunder like the cities of ash for their lack of charity.

For it was in his power to say the word and all we have known would have been engulfed in fire and flame. Instead, he has left us both to honor him while he does what he must. Remember, Peter, that the rock must yield to the four winds! Listen with your heart as well as your ears. Listen now, Peter! All is forgiven." She let go his beard and the gaze she had locked upon his eyes and as she turned toward Yehuda and the boats, Miryam said once more, "Go home."

"My lady," Yehuda gestured to Miryam and without resignation she took his outstretched hand and boarded the craft. The men heaved their oars as Miryam kept her sight upon the ship and dusted off her sandals. Peter sat from where he stood and wept.

# ~ Chapter 8 ~

# Sailing Away

*"He stilled the storm to a whisper; the waves of the sea were hushed. They were glad when it grew calm, and he guided them to their desired haven."*
*~Psalm 107:29-30*

Yehuda stood there at the bow of the beached craft that would lead them to the ship. The road to the shores of their new life seemed long, yet they knew the rest of their journey would be longer. His mother's family of Arimathea had always been generous and held their wealth quite secure. While Miryam stood on the waterfront with Simon Peter, Yehuda took stock of the journey's supplies that were being ushered to the ship for them. Fingers of Creation stretched down upon their head from this overcast day. Perhaps it was him reaching out to those he loved one more time.

Standing in his tortured silence, feeling the need to say something to someone, Yehuda struck up awkward conversations with the rowers that would ferry them to their faithful vessel. He studied the ship from the shore as if remembering the decks of another vessel he and his brothers had ferried across Galilee. One of the oarsmen placed a hand on Yehuda's shoulder, startling him, "No worries, Sir. She will treat your family with respect and carry you safely to any distant shores you choose. Her inner rooms will keep you and your family safe." This oarsman seemed to know the passengers he would be transporting a little more than Yehuda was comfortable, yet Yosef held great strength in Jerusalem, and perhaps his mind was just a bit too paranoid for his own good. Being out in public was not an easy thing for him right now, and it put the family in danger.

"He will keep us all safe in the storms we encounter." Yehuda replied. Many of those squalls Yeshua slept through to the amazement of the others. They all doubted the happenings around them at times, yet they always knew the calm within every storm was only moments away. This calm, however, only seemed to foreshadow a life of flare-ups.

Yehuda shouted, "Miryam!" from the stillness of his mind as he would often do for Yeshua, yet the stares from the distant shadows still plagued his understanding. The distraction had toned down his ability to speak to another's mind. His thoughts, however, continued, "Let Peter go. We must carry on as Brother asked of us. Those we leave behind may have much on their minds right now, however we may draw the attention of some who still wait in the shadows." He felt an awkward stare pierce his attention from behind him in one of the boats, and the scar on his cheek stung with alarm.

"Remember, my brother. Patience is a skill you truly must learn."

There was always an inner voice Yehuda could rely on to voice his frustrations. "Must I always stand ready? Must I always be waiting for…"

The response wasn't coming from within this time. "Breathe, brother. Simply breathe. The storm of time will always crash against the bow of your ship.

There is nothing you can do. She has much she needs to unburden from her heart, as does he." The words came not simply as a memory, yet more as they used to when they were young – a true voice only heard in the trained recesses of the mind. Not always needing lip and tongue to discourse the meanings in their thoughts, a glance sometimes held more discussion. Yeshua's physical shell no longer needed sustenance – surely that barrier being removed made his messages easier to convey – at least to those who have an ear.

Yehuda believed he would hear much from his brother now without the intruding ears of others. They often struggled for time to sit and talk together outside of the trained maternal ears now on the shore with Peter. Often the heart can also feel the vibrations of the tongue of the mind.

Miryam turned toward him as if to stir the winds for the sails that had yet to unfurl. As if also meant for Yehuda, his ears caught what his heart had yearned "All is forgiven...Go home," is all he heard as she turned from Peter's tearing and saddened countenance. A great weight was removed from Yehuda's shoulders. Had she truly forgiven him as well as Peter? Amongst the twelve, there was much jealousy and spiteful things said over the years concerning Yeshua's relationship with Miryam. Many of them left their families behind, while others flourished in their familial prosperity. Yehuda had never found time to garner any sort of healthy relationship with anyone besides his brother – and at times even that lacked health and vitality.

Where would home be for them now? Who would take in this family? Surely some of the contacts that they had made over the years spent traveling with

Yosef of Arimathea would be welcoming and useful in their journeys. They were to set sail for distant lands; the galleys would be well stocked for a lengthy trip for the edges of the sea unknown to their feet. Might they step on the shores of greener locations? Possibly a home rich with timber; or possibly enough land for sheep and goats? A home where that auburn hair and those olive eyes do not look so out of place! Perhaps in the coming years, they too would reconcile their hidden emotions, trapped down deep for myriad of reasons, for the sake of the children. For the sake of the one they both truly loved.

Again from some unseen corner of the psyche, "Look to the skies always, brother. I will be there to guide you. You will come across many different lands in your travels. I only hope you find the peace you have always sought. I … will…" Even now, from the ethers of creation, Yeshua stammered when emotion got the best of him, or maybe it was something best said in the embrace of their minds without words.

"I… will miss you too, my brother. Yet I have many faces and tongues surrounding me to remind me of you." As tears welled up in Yehuda's eyes, Miryam stepped from the shore, took her husband's hand and sat beside Elisheva. One more glance toward Brother Peter, and back to her husband's twin. Now her husband…

That voice from within crept into the conversation in the shock that both Yehuda and Miryam were both now feeling. "Her… husband. Husband?" His hands so wished to cover his face at the thought of the long travels ahead of them, and of the long walks they would have on foreign soils in the years ahead; if he had, doubt would surely encroach her mind. Or were they truly embarking on a new life together in which neither of them knew what to expect?

"All is forgiven…" kept running through his mind as the boats began their way to the ship. He was anxious to get going, and his hastening actions, rushing the children onto the boat, and hurrying them to their quarters began to task Miryam's mind. He could feel her, and the memories of the tightening noose from which Peter had saved him became more intense as the burn around his neck seemed to tingle. They were as vivid as the flames of anger or some directed emotion that was being shot his way from a girl who could easily be described as another Miryam. With an understanding smile felt from the disembodied voice of his brother in his mind, "Be careful of the fire in those eyes, brother. They will either warm your heart or singe the hairs on your beard!"

"Indeed!" was all he could think of. "Brother, leave us to our storms and foreign shores, yet never leave my mind. I dare not think of a time when you will not be within my soul. Your flesh is gone, I made sure of that, as you requested. No one will find the bones to control your spirit. Though you may visit many in foreign lands, as we shall visit many and share the teachings you so easily understood, never leave our minds and hearts. I cannot bear this new life without your presence around us."

A great sigh came on the winds as the last of the voyage preparations were completed. Knowing he would never see these lands again, he turned to look upon them once more. The sigh from the winds came again, together with more from Yeshua, "I will always be with you, brow to brow and heart to heart. We shared the same home before we broke the door of life into this world, and we shared much of our early years. You also spent much time alone, and thought only of yourself a great deal. Be sure to think of others now, brother, and share the good times and the bad times with all you meet. The entire story is what you will live, and what you will tell. It matters not who will hear or listen. It is the telling of the story that is important."

Yehuda's attention was brought to the other ships he could see. "Many will not believe you, yet in the end of the age I will also come to you again. I will remind you of these times so that everyone may know the Truth. My words are eternal, yet as a means of control, I never want them to be used. A man comes soon to turn our knowing and the words I ministered to the benefit of those who line his coffers. Some things we cannot control, yet many will have an ear to hear and an eye to see at the end of the age."

Yehuda could still feel stares from the shadows, "Let the words of the Deceiver be heard as he will try to deceive, yet in that attempt many will still hear my heart. Let them see our days, hear our words and know the Truth as it surely was."

"How will they hear? How will they see?" Like his Abba, sometimes Yehuda needed more information than simply knowing it will come to pass.

"When the age comes to a close, look to the science the Nazarene taught us. Look to the spheres and hold close to your heart Miryam's brother. He will be sharing all the knowledge of the coming Age of Great Light on the words of the wind. His family has and always will be blessed, and will share his great affluence with those he knows in his soul. He sacrificed his head so that the body of his family will always be safe for many generations to come. Holy waters created by the murmurs of the Angels will herald the new age and the time when I will see you again."

Yeshua's voice began to turn to a whisper as if distance from the Holy Land put distance between them, yet the heart of his brother would always speak loud and strong regardless of distance. "Go now and share our times with everyone you meet. I love you, brother. More than anyone will ever understand or care to understand. You are my heart and my mind. We were of one design and still are. We are one, no longer concerned with the timing of our entrances. We... are... one."

~~~

The ship had been away from the shores of the lands they knew as home for only a short time. The children had been tended to their every need by Miryam. Yehuda sat staring out to the horizon, envisioning the times that were ahead of them. He began to think to himself, "What are we doing? Where are we going? Perhaps..."

"Perhaps Cypress, Yehuda." A gentle hand rested on his left shoulder. "He often spoke of you wanting to go there. Both of you liked the distant shores and far off lands when you traveled with your Uncle Yosef." The words were soft, and somewhat enchanting. Miryam knew her place as was prescribed by the Law. Yehuda was her husband now, and that she would honor for all her days.

Yehuda spun, startled by her gentle assurances. "Um, yes. Indeed we did." He stiffened and turned his back on her, not with intent of disrespect, yet more of reaction to the electricity he felt that seemed to sting him. He knew her intent was to calm the stormy waters between them.

"Husband and brother you are to me, Yehuda. I meant what I said to Peter. All is forgiven. The hard glances, ardent stares and implications over the years…"

"Speak no more of it, Miryam." It was too soon to begin another journey. This one had just begun. "We have many times ahead of us to work this out. I heard you while we were waiting for you."

"The folly of impatience will only bring you down again, Yehuda." The words Yeshua spoke to her were still fresh in her mind.

Spinning around, holding her by the shoulders, and knowing he could be sent over the rails at any minute, he felt the need to assert his place, "Woman. We have both witnessed things we never thought or imagined would transpire as quickly as they did. Could I simply have some time to put a few pieces together? I have no family with me anymore outside of you and the children. My mother and father were left behind with all the comforts that could temper the storm in my mind."

She could have been shocked, angered, and any number of reactionary emotions would have been justified. However, Miryam had a knowing of her own, and she knew the temper Yehuda would always have inside of him. Perhaps a simple reminder from Mother Miriam would be sufficient to calm his storms. "Indeed.

Husband. Your Ima told me many stories of your youth. And the children have always loved the telling of the days when their Father and their Uncle were young. Would you join us in our quarters?"

Reclaiming a more stoic façade, Yehuda played along with Miryam's decision. "Fine, my lady. Ima would often over embellish the stories of our beginnings. Both of you could weave such wonderful tapestries."

"Wonderful! Children?" she cried as she excitedly led Yehuda into their quarters, pulling him along by the hand. Yehuda wondered where this excitement could be coming from. How could she switch from being the grieving wife to the excited teenager she had not been for years? The fire in her heart would stoke many new experiences for sure.

"Children, Yehuda would like to hear the stories that Savta would tell about Father's and Uncle's beginning. Do you not, Yehuda?" She turned with a look of both excitement and pointed direction for Yehuda to also be excited, as if to stir the excitement of the children, "Do you not? Yehuda?"

Attempting to mask any sarcasm in his response, "Oh, yes! Of course. Do tell, Miryam." Calling each their names in front of the children made sense, yet how would this be perceived in new lands. Maybe it would matter nothing to strangers. Yehuda had considered Yeshua's children as his own for years now. It would be only the difference in their minds that would be seen if they let show. But even the best laid plans…

# ~ Chapter 9 ~

# The Plan

*"Oh, that my words were recorded, that they were written on a scroll, that they were inscribed with an iron tool on lead, or engraved in rock forever!"*
*~ Job 19:23-24*

"What troubles you, Brother?" His hand rested on Yehuda's shoulder as if nothing of significance had been discussed.

Yeshua was the one who broke the door into this life and Yehuda's logic followed this scriptural understanding, "'So the last will be first, and the first will be last'. That is how it was meant to be!" He had understood that since he was last to enter this world, he should be the first to leave.

"I will abandon all of you? You tell them all that you will leave them? Let it be me that takes your place instead." It was known that those not liked by the Sanhedrin often found themselves within unfortunate circumstances – such as choking on a bone or falling from a cot in such a way that one would break their own neck as they rose in the morning. The crime of working on the Sabbath, of which Yeshua was accused, warranted no more than censure from speaking in the Temple. Yet who knew what stones they would cast instead.

The plan had been set in place. Yeshua knew that the Sanhedrin may not directly attack the families, yet something worse would happen to them if he did not drink this cup. He could not allow it. He needed his friends, his disciples, to keep watch over his wife and children, his mother and father.

"My friends, those whom I love so, we celebrate the Seder tonight. Yet, tonight I tell you that I will abandon all of you." Yeshua could see the shock on their faces.

It was Simon the Zealot that said, "Surely, Lord, you would not do that! You would not abandon all of us."

Yeshua raised his hand to calm their excitement, "So that my family can be safe, so that all of you can be saved from the Sanhedrin and their agenda…"

Peter interrupted, "What could they possibly levy against you? You healed a lame man on the Sabbath. Your only crime was to tell a paralyzed man, who was now fully healed, to carry his mat. Surely the miraculous work is greater than the ridiculous letter of the Law."

Stoically Yeshua rose from his seat, "Yet the Law is what we live by, and I accept the punishment." Yeshua walked to the eastern window.

Peter followed him, grabbing him respectfully to gain his attention, "Yet, Master, you speak of your blood and your body as if they will stone you! Yet, what stone would not bounce from your flesh?"

Matthew exclaimed, "The crime is theirs with their lack of charity and jealousy!"

Andrew added, "They're jealous of your ability to draw people to your words on a simple hillside. They can't even garner enough people to warrant opening the Temple when it's required of them!"

Yeshua returned to the table to explain the danger that loomed upon all of them. "The ones who should be teaching the way of charity are instead the ones that defile the gift of life. They demand that one purchase a living thing, and then the priest kills it and proclaims that the Lords on High are pleased with their burnt offerings. They perpetuate a vicious cycle with the merchants in the Temples. Repentance is free. They killed Yohanan for speaking the Truth, and challenging traditions that do not make sense in accordance with the Law. They know I see the Truth of their darkened lives and that I will be the one to bring it crumbling down around them. This is why they seek me out and this is why I must save you from the same fate. Yet, I promise you, I will return to you. However, for some time I must go to rebuild a proper Temple."

Yeshua knew the only way to continue their mission, and to save those whom he loved from impending destruction, was to offer up his life.

Simon questioned Yeshua's decisions, "But, Master, why send Yehuda to the priests; why not one of Barabbas' boys?"

Yeshua knew they were clouded by their fear of being without him. "Knowing that the Romans have taken Barabbas in answer to the latest rebellion, we must not risk the associations that would further jeopardize our freedoms."

While they were all arguing Yeshua's decisions, Yosef of Arimathea and Nicodemus began the rumors in the Council which would make it plausible for Yehuda to appear and offer up his own brother to qualify for his greater inheritance. The rumor must give the impression that there was a sense of animosity between the brothers, and they knew this was something that the Sanhedrin would utilize.

Satisfied he would reign in his own tempers this time, Yeshua was not so sure about the reactions of those around him. If they pulled him from the house or arrested him in the street without warning, a riot cold ensue. If they tried to protect him by the sword, his life may be spared but all would be doomed. Yeshua could not bear to see those whom he loved so dearly – his wife and children, his parents and his dearest friends – witness such possible horror and what it would do to them. If they used Yosef and Nicodemus to control the timing in which Yeshua was to be arrested, they could make sure it would be arranged for the rest to be saved from retribution or additional casualties.

Although many of the disciples wanted to accompany Yeshua to the garden at Gethsemane, Yeshua would only allow John, who was not married, Simon Peter whose family lived far from the district, and his cousin James whose family was grown and would be safe in the protection of the house of Arimathea.

Yehuda was the only one that Yeshua could trust to accomplish this. It was known for some time that Yeshua and his brother had clearer communication between the two of them than anyone could understand. Perhaps it was because of their shared heart. This incredible knowing between Yeshua and Yehuda would act as a silent alarm to put into place what needed to be done in those final moments.

~~~

Yeshua had been taken into custody by Caiaphas and his gang. As Yeshua had feared, even his most trusted disciples resorted to the base emotions in their distress. The guard had witnessed the miracles of the extraordinary gifts Yeshua had been blessed with from the Lords on High. Even here, in the dank and wretched conditions of the cell they had thrown him in, the moonlight cast a ray of illumination. Yeshua reached out again to Yehuda.

Betrayed, Yehuda had only run a short distance, unable to drag himself away from watching secretly the brutality of the long walk to the death chamber he knew awaited his brother. He was no threat to the Romans, so their brutal sentencing was not a concern. However, the Sanhedrin wanted Yeshua completely silenced. There was a thick presence in the air that reminded Yehuda of his former demons who were always hell-bent on destruction and chaos. He could feel the stares all around him.

Gravely disappointed in Yeshua's change of their secret plans, Yehuda conveyed his anguish through their private communication, "I never thought this would have happened, Yeshua. This was not the plan!"

Yeshua simply said, "It was the plan everyone else knew."

"I would lead them to you. In the darkened light of the gardens they would see me kiss you. With that signal they would know it was you. They would trust the scar to identify me from you, which you were to change through illusion. Yet that is not what you did!" Yehuda could feel a place he had not touched before inside Yeshua's mind. It echoed the sense of dread he felt all around him in the garden, while Yeshua lay in the damp recesses of the Sanhedrin's confines.

"It was not," was all Yeshua could say.

"Now you are in their midst. They can do whatever they wish to you now. They are abominable asps who would poison their own blood for their rise to power!"

"And now all of you are safe," was all Yeshua could say.

Yehuda pushed all that he could, "You were to continue the ministry on to all the peoples of the world, and I would…" Dismissing the words Yeshua seemed to be ignoring, Yehuda continued ever so snidely, "Pay it no mind, Yeshua, your will is done. When you set your mind to something, it's always just that – done." Those words, which he forced himself to say, left a bad taste in his mouth. He rose from the ground in the moonlight.

That same moonlight Yeshua now found as convenient means of transportation to be with his brother one last time. Yeshua knew what was going to happen and he needed his brother, yet Yehuda found the flames of disappointment a quick element rushing his blood to boil. Yeshua's body lay seeming lifeless on the cold floor of the dungeon. Yet Yeshua found himself standing behind Yehuda.

Yehuda turned to follow the winds into the night. Yehuda's eyes found a quiet spot to find the answers to his bothered heart, and he headed toward that point.

This change in events, this act of betrayal, Yeshua knew his brother would have trouble accepting. They needed to be in agreement with this alteration in the plan. What Yehuda hadn't known, and could not be told, was that it was not the will of Yeshua's that existed as the issue now.

Grasping eagerly for his brother's arm, "Yehuda, your heart is so heavy…" Yehuda darted away from his touch. He was shocked by his own vision. Was Yeshua truly standing there with him or had he begun to go mad? The surprise lasted only a moment in his mounting anger.

Yeshua continued even in Yehuda's astonishment, "I hesitate to think how you will be able to sail across the seas with our family. Carry not any burden from our lives on your heart. We all have done things…"

Had his anger created his own apparition to unleash his ruefulness? "I am no longer concerned about the things that I have done," indignantly casting Yeshua's hand behind him.

This needed to be settled. "Yehuda! Come back here! We are not done with this!" Commanding others was a power the two never had over each other. Yehuda hesitated to see what his brother wanted, even though he would have none of it right now. All Yeshua wanted was his brother's embrace.

Spinning around and hurrying to the stalwart countenance he wore lately, Yehuda pressed nose to nose and toe to toe with Yeshua, looking him straight in those amber eyes with the depth and conviction of a legion of soldiers as the fury leapt out, "You may command the clay birds to fly, devils to be gone, the dead to rise, the gnats to bother another and that woman to bear you children, yet you have never commanded me, Yeshua! Just let me go be alone for a while. I need to think." Spinning back toward that silent spot to reflect without his thoughts being intruded upon by even his twin, Yehuda headed toward the darkness.

Yearning for his brother to simply understand all that had transpired as the way it had to be, Yeshua desperately reached out, "Yehuda, please!" Yehuda continued to storm off.

Yehuda knew they would find each other after they had their time alone. They always were able with the knowing they shared, the connection of mind and body they had since birth, to be assured they would see each other again soon. Yehuda truly needed to think and find some reprieve in the darkness of this night.

Speaking to the self within, Yehuda could have very well been seen as mentally deficient, talking to himself and waving his arms around in a conversation with no one. "He claims to know the burdens on my heart? Burdens they are indeed! Burdens collected in a ship bound for lands unknown and staring at me, a man who is not their father, and from a woman who knows more than she should! Yet the love he has for her I know too. Yet that is his cup to drink from, not mine."

Yehuda shouted to the winds for even the King to hear, "So the last will be first, and the first will be last? That is how it was meant to be! Pray to the Lord or whatever angelic wing keeps you safe, Brother!" As he turned around to shout at Yeshua, he found that he was no longer there.

He threw his arms up in a sense of surrender or defeat, waving it all away. Continuing to talk to no one but himself, he faded into the obscurity of the night, leaving his brother to the fading light that had taken Yeshua back to his confines where the Sanhedrin had left him.

~~~

In the darkness, aspects of Yehuda's consciousness struck up a conversation and a sense of a battle between the facets of his psyche.

"Shall I blame the weaver for the transgressions embroidered on my tapestry, when I am the one who made the decisions?"

"What was it that turned the hand of destiny from where it was only moments before?"

Before him tumbled the sack full of silver coins the Sanhedrin had given to him; even in the night, each silver coin struck a light from the distance and pierced Yehuda's self, "Look at these ugly pieces of greed! The hands that struck these had no ill intent when making them. There is no fault placed in the hands of the one who twisted the silver into coin. The burden sits in the heart of the one that placed the purchase price on these simple, inanimate pieces of material tender. If I were paid to purchase sica from the smith down the road, am I to blame for the life it extinguishes?"

"What was it that turned his hand? It pains me to think of the reasons behind our actions. Yet if it is his will for it to be done, then so be it."

"I learned a very long time ago to just trust in him."

"Father had trust in him – he always trusted in the guidance of our Lord even when sanity told him to run."

"What key was in the lock of his mind in that cold winter air so long ago? There was no shelter but his faith with the stinging elements."

"Stop asking that question! What key? What key?"

"Surely, Ima had plenty, yet they were forced to hide in the squalor of the caves. No matter the ego placed in other's actions, those means and measures are for them to turn in their mind."

"It was that hand of brotherhood on my shoulder that plagues my mind now. Not the words of adoration, if indeed they were truly words of such. There must be an answer to the question as to who will be blamed for this. Yet, what is it that brings peace in the actions soon to be played out?"

"Questions, misconceptions, misunderstandings, denials, grief – these are all heavy stones. All possibly to be flung our way for this. They all sit in there, in that room, not knowing why, contemplating the day to come, and we sit here alone in the darkness and wonder about our own self. A decision must have been made somewhere."

"We all talk and preach of Creation's power and the wonder held in our hands every second of every day. Yet do we truly know the power of that hand as it swings through the midst of our minds, and our lives?

"What more drives a man to act in the middle of inaction or controversy as when absolutely nothing is being done around him besides chatter? Yet when something is done, is it the right something? Was it the right thing to do? Will it be the right thing?"

Yehuda's mind raced with the possibilities. All of his selves attempting to make some sense of an understanding of what was transpiring asked, "What if this is done, instead of that?"

"If I throw a rock in the water, what ripple will it cause in the next village? Oh, the injury this decision could cause if it falls short. The emissary is always liable for the intentions others do observe."

The selves began to coalesce and become one again. Something was setting in; something of an understanding. "Perhaps we allow the past to be our guide. What would Yeshua do?"

Yehuda wiped countless tears from his face as he prayed for the salvation of those who would prefer to see his blood spilled. He had heard the torment of the mind as peaceful words were uttered to a rioting crowd. He knew the anguish behind the choices he made. "He knew the love in this heart as he casted away my demons."

With his arms outstretched, his head cocked back, he posed his questions to the stars. With a flash, a light went streaking across the masterpiece of the cosmos painted above him. He needed to ask for answers. He collapsed to his knees in prayer.

The light beamed down on both of them. Yeshua prayed facing the Eastern skies for guidance, "What is it that drives us to make the choices? There are countless elements within each option – faith, knowledge, influence, compulsion, circumstances, and demands. Again, what is it that turns the hand on the key?"

Yehuda prayed into the light coming from the West, "Whose hand is it turning that crucial element of thought into decision – from decision to plan, from plan to action, or from action to history? That initial decision had questions, and those early questions surely had lasting and final, exacting answers. Yet, who turns those answers into actions?" Desperation came to his voice, "Which action do we take?"

As if hearing his brother's prayer, Yeshua bowed his head to his chest saying with such justification and faith-filled acceptance, "Leap and you will fly, brother!"

Yehuda heard an answer in his mind, to which he returned, "Sometimes there is no time for calculation, just action. Yet, what do I do?"

He cried out to Yeshua again, "Yeshua. How will all these events be seen? Is this just happening to us or will the world see all that is transpiring?"

"Dearest brother, who will believe any story of truth as it stands? With each retelling of any happening, the story will change. You are who you are. I am who I am. Our lives are what they are. Remember our lessons with Barabbas as we studied the brightest stars? Look to the skies. This is not our home."

"Yeshua? When all is done, who will believe the truth?"

"Indeed, Yehuda. Who will believe the truth?"

# ~ Chapter 10 ~

# The Announcements

*"And Mary replied to him, I see two people with mine eyes, the one weeping and mourning, the other laughing and rejoicing." ~ The Protevangelion 12:9*

For many nights, Zecharias did not sleep. His rest was filled with fitful dreams and during his days at the temple, he staggered in the perfumed air, seeing shadows and images in the smoky rooms. His mind raced and his heartbeat pounded like that of a hare in flight. His thoughts dwelled upon the words he heard both within his chamber and within his mind.

Elsbeth kneeled at his side, his head upon the thick planked table. "What troubles you, husband?" He looked down into her eyes and wept into her arms.

"All these years, I have wanted a son. A child to carry on in the temple. I am old. We should be seeing our grandchildren now married. Yet, these last nights, I have been awakened to the voice that speaks of our son, one that is yet to come – that he will be known in the House of the Lord for all generations yet to come." He expected Elsbeth to reproach his statement yet instead she reached up and stroked the waves of his hair, then she kissed the tract of tears on each cheek and his closed eyelids gently.

"No, Zecharias, I am the one that should be crying. I have not given you that son that we both have wanted." She paused and waited for him to open his eyes and look at her. There he saw the glimmer of understanding, the shining eyes of hope and joy. "Come from the table, Zecharias. It is late and morning is nigh. I, too, have dreamed."

~~~

Soon word arrived to Joachim that Elsbeth was with child. Joachim read the message over and over to Hannah, noting the same images that his daughter had just shared of the bright light and soft voice. Elspeth asked for Miriam to come and assist her in running the household. Joachim and Hannah gathered provisions for the journey while Miriam spoke with Yosef. She would tell him of her encounter with the Great Light.

Yosef shook with rage after Miriam explained her vision. "How is this possible, Miriam? Either you laid down with a man or you did not! If you carry a child then you have shamed me and you have shamed our families! Who is this vile man that would take one that is betrothed? If this has just occurred, how would you know you carry a child?" His questions rattled off like his chisel upon the stone.

Miriam kept her countenance smooth and her voice just as sweet. "Who am I to question the will of the Most High? I have told you the truth, Yosef. I have told you of a great miracle. I will go to the home of my mother's kinswoman. She, too, carries a child though she has been barren. I will not shame your house or mine but bring it glory. I am simply a handmaid of the Lord. If you think of me otherwise, then the shame is already yours." She turned on her heel and made way to leave. Yosef took her by the shoulder, turned her face to his and simply looked into her bold eyes.

"Miriam, they will stone you for certain," he whispered. Although his face still burned, Yosef knew from her eyes that Miriam believed what she had just told him. The rage melted away to sadness and to fear.

She did not pull away. "I will see to Elsbeth. It is many a day's walk. I am not known in her village, nor will I share my good tidings with another. My mother and father have provided for my journey there."

~~~

For many nights did Yosef consider the situation. The curse upon his line had kept him from seeking a wife. Then, that young man hired him for work in one of the high houses near Jerusalem. Who knew what prompted Yosef to choose him!

His disgrace, his shame! To be granted such a wife! And now, this waking dream was seared into his mind!

If only Miriam would forgive him!

# ~ Chapter 11 ~

# The Halting of Time

*"Hear the word of the LORD, you nations; proclaim it in distant coastlands: 'He who scattered Israel will gather them and will watch over his flock like a shepherd.'"* ~ *Jeremiah 31:10*

And when she could travel no further, she bade Yosef to make way to the cliffside and there was found a smooth crevice in which she could shelter for her time was near. Yosef ran to seek out a midwife and in his quick passage was slow to observe the frank stillness about him. The shepherds with their rods extended toward the also motionless sheep, the kids stiffened as their leap was held to the ground, the courtyards silenced in mid-bite at the evening meal. It was not until he saw the woman running towards him, her eyes wide that he noticed he outpaced the travelers on ass and foot with ease.

The woman ran to him and exclaimed, "Are you the one who seeks a mid-wife?"

"Yes, yes," Yosef replied and she followed him directly as he ran back to the resting place. It was then that Yosef saw that those on the road and those in the fields and those in the huts made no movement yet his heart and his body raced toward Miriam. The woman stifled her groans as they made way past each caravan until they reached the path to the mouth of the cave.

It was near dusk yet the evening shone here as mid-day. As Yosef and the woman made the small climb, the sound of the chiming of bells filled the air. Yosef fell to his knees as he came to the side of Miriam, her face wrought with tears and joy. Already wrapped in her veil slept her first born son and at her breast did she give suck to his twin.

The woman ushered Yosef to the tethered donkey for the blanket and their provisions. He gathered all that he could and placed them down by the woman's instruction. She wiped the face of Miriam with her own veil and kissed her unbound hair. "I am Adelai and an angel of light bid me from my table here. Do you claim both of these babes at this hour?" When Miriam consented to claim both, Adelai smiled and began her work of washing each child and trimming their navel strings, returning them to their mother's blanket as she assisted Miriam in her washing and changing of garments. All the while, the babes made no cry.

When all was prepared, Adelai called to Yosef from his supplications. Although the sun had since set, the clouds up above still shone with great light.

Yosef knelt at the edge of the blanket that held the three before him. He looked into the face of this young woman who yet again had surprised him in her steadfast and calming nature. As if struck dumb, he spoke no word yet his eyes held all the questions.

Miriam smiled at him and reached for his hand. He did not pull away. "This," she said as she touched his hand to the babe closest to him, "is Yeshua, the first born, the one who will redeem Israel from destruction. And this," as she placed his fingers unto the second child, "is Yehuda. I have brought him also to my breast. He, too, will watch over the children of Israel. I have claimed them both."

Yosef sat for a moment longer in silence. Adelai scarcely took in breath as the moment elapsed. In the shining cloud light, Yosef took up the infant Yeshua and held him up over his head. "This is my charge and my son, Yeshua." He placed the swaddled infant into Miriam's arms. He then took up the second child and held him at arm's reach. Adelai felt her body tense as Yosef stood up with this infant until he proclaimed, "This is my charge and my son, Yehuda. Unless the Almighty take him from my hands now, no man shall cast him to Sheol. This, I promise."

Adelai sunk to the ground in amazement as the ringing of the bells became song. When she recovered, the night was deep yet still the silver clouds gave light to the small rock chamber. As the clouds dispersed, she heard the clamoring of hoof and footfalls along the cliff-side path. Herding unblemished lambs and kids, shepherds dedicated offerings to where the light had led them.

# ~ Chapter 12 ~

# A Stranger in Town

*"After Jesus was born in Bethlehem in Judea, during the time of King Herod, Magi from the east came to Jerusalem and asked, 'Where is the one who has been born king of the Jews? We saw his star in the east, and have come to worship him.'"*
*~ Matthew 2:1-2*

There were Kingdoms of men in many lands who studied the stars and the movements of the heavens. Their tribes were wealthy; they wore fine linens and silks of renowned intricacy. They harnessed beasts of enormous size with fangs the length of most men and allowed apes to be the stewards of their temples. They performed the magic of the ancient Pharaohs and so were greatly feared and mistrusted.

A great caravan arrived in the territory of the Herod and, by request, was escorted by the guard, reached the palace near the time of the harvest. Three representatives and their viziers presented Herod with caskets of jeweled gold, and resins and medicines of their countries.

They inquired of Herod of the great light they had seen in the heavens and of the city it had illuminated not far off from the palace. They told him of the spinning merkaba of golden light that had appeared to each of them in their own locations, and, announcing in a voice that came from every corner of their own apartment, the arrival of a King above all Kings that was born into the people which Herod ruled. They told of how the star had led them to one another in their respective travels to come and pay homage to the newborn king and how the star had let them now to Herod. Herod kept his face smooth when they asked to be brought to the child who they supposed would be of his line.

Herod, who had casted his seed casually for his own delight, contemplated now this issue. He would not let the product of a common whore usurp his throne. Quickly he concocted a plan of his own.

He had recognized the description of the place where the child was born, a nearby city known as Bethlehem. He knew of prophesies of the city of David. He would stop at nothing to see them unfulfilled in his days. He would find the child through the census and destroy it and the whore.

With a mock smile, he addressed the powerful visitors. "No, the child does not reside here yet. But go, and present him your gifts and urge his mother to return so that he may receive the finest education and learn the workings of ruling the Kingdom so all will know him from his infancy."

In Herod's attempt to win favor, after a banquet in their honor, the visitors and their caravans departed towards Bethlehem escorted by his chief guards. In the night, the flashing star appeared again from the heavens and the echoes of its voice boomed in the ears of the guards. Upon hearing the words that described Herod as the murdering tyrant that they well knew, the young men ran off, leaving the caravans and their posts. The price of their betrayal to Herod would be small in comparison to the price of forever that this voice would exact.

In the days to come, Yosef heard the talk of the caravans and was afraid. He finished his work quickly and returned to his home that he shared with his brother and his family. Miriam rarely emerged from the courtyard and into the streets as many had mocked her and the children and pitied Yosef for the woe that had befallen him, as word had spread of the two infants that she fed at her breasts.

Yosef met Miriam in the meager garden where the boys slept under the shade of the olive tree, never out of her sight. Yosef told her of the story he had heard and how from the wall he could see their numbers and heard their drums and the clanging of their symbols. He recalled to her the rumor of their magic and how they came to salute the new King born in Bethlehem, especially how those who told the story had laughed, not knowing his line, that maybe they would see King David take up the throne again.

Miriam's eyes widened and she shook from fear. "Yosef, we must run or surely they will slay them both with the power of their magics." Yosef agreed yet was also fearful that if they ran now, all would point in their direction and there would be no protection from the slow death of the cold outside of the wall of their own people.

Miriam took up the babes in her arms and told Yosef, "It is true what they say. What woe has befallen you!" Yosef smiled so broadly that his teeth shined a beam that slowed even her tears. It was often that his brow was furrowed but rare that he would smile great enough that it could be determined through his beard.

"The only woe I shall ever know is when I am away from you." He tenderly kissed each child and then most sympathetically kissed her cheeks and brushed away her tears. "Let us trust in the Lord. Surely he did not bring us thus far to destroy us. Come, let us go inside and speak on this with Zebedee." After long discussion, it was agreed that Miriam and Yosef would keep shelter with those who loved them and those who would defend all who lived in this home with words and flesh and blood.

Two days hence, at breakfast, came a light knocking at the door so that it was scarcely heard. Zebedee opened the door to find what appeared to be nothing more than a tall beggar, covered and hooded in threadbare and patched common cloak with layers of dirt about its hem. His face was hidden in the hood yet, if one looked closely, could see through the thin cloth of the sleeve, the glint of something in the slant of the morning sun. The low timbered voice, in an almost whisper asked in an elegant diction of Aramaic, "Brother, would thee bid me welcome?"

Yosef's brother, entranced by the lilt of the voice, welcomed the stranger and insisted to him to take breakfast with them. The stranger, still in his cloak, with Yosef's brother ushering him in, went into the courtyard where the family was assembled. All at the same instant, with surprise and amazement, remained as still as the painted walls of Egypt as the stranger removed his cloak.

The tall stranger was as dark as the midnight sky when it carried the rain, his ebony hair cropped close upon his head, and though old enough, had no trace of a beard. His robes were sown through with gold and with silver, jewels flashed and reflected in every direction. Great rings bedecked his graceful fingers and his ears were banded in the same manner. His eyes, however, shone with such brightness like the great lions, even in the darkness, that the glint of gold adornments paled in comparison.

When no one stirred, the stranger slowly looked about those sitting for their meal and those who stood with the platters of bread and cheese and who dared not move. He looked upon each of them in turn until his eyes fell upon Miriam, one child suckling at her breast and its twin sprawled over her knee. Before Yosef could move to block them from this stranger's view, the ebony man smiled broadly and said in his lyrical voice, "Hail, Miriam! Hail, Yosef, of the line of David! I have come from afar to bid thee greetings and to honor these, thy children, for which you have been most greatly blessed. May the Light ever shine upon you."

Yosef, who had been stiffened in fear, now felt the same calmness as when the angel, who called himself GabriEl, had spoken to him in both times of dream and when he toiled alone. Without hesitation, Yosef bid his nephew to hurry and bring the carpet so that their guest may be seated without spoiling his robe. The stranger placed his hand upon the arm of the boy as he rose and told him to sit, and gathering the exceptional robes about him, sat upon the bare swept stone.

Zebedee offered up prayers for their meal and then had his eldest hold out a bowl of water and their best towel to the stranger, who in turn washed his hands and his face. Later, after breakfast, the women remarked that the towel smelled of perfume – that indeed it was fresher after the stranger wiped his hand upon it than before. In silence, they ate their bread and the wet cheese and the few olives that were to be had.

After some time, it was Miriam who spoke and although all of Yosef's household was shocked, none were surprised by her boldness. "Stranger, you have called me by name, yet I know not yours. Do tell us who you may be and why it is you know my name."

## ~ Chapter 13 ~

## You Must Go

*"When they had gone, an angel of the Lord appeared to Joseph in a dream. "Get up," he said, "take the child and his mother and escape to Egypt. Stay there until I tell you, for Herod is going to search for the child to kill him." ~ Matthew 2:13*

The stranger finished his mouthful and drank his cup of water, placing it gently down upon the planks of the table. He smoothed the generous folds of his robe on his lap and began, "I am called Melchior in my kingdom, in lands not unlike your own. My people descended from lines of great seers and wisdom keepers, like those you call prophets and physicians. We are a peaceful people, and unlike the Pharaohs of the Egyptians who enslaved your people, our Kinsmen strive to find peace with one another. Our lands are dotted with stones that others relish, and our fields are filled with goodness to eat. We are a rich people in our heritage as well as what we offer in trade. Our people travel the roads beyond Syria to the lands below Egypt. That is whom I represent as a leader of my Kingdom and how it is I have come to know your names." He paused for a moment, looking at the faces filled with awe at the beggar who was welcomed to their table, for now they knew they sat in audience of a King.

Yosef shifted as if to speak yet Melchior continued on, "My friends, we have come far from our homes, my companions and I, to offer our gifts to the newborn King; the one who will be a savior to all our people, to the tribes that were scattered in ages past to all the lands. The redeemer of all those who strive to keep the law of Kindness was promised to each tribe. From the heavens, we were given a sign that he is born unto you, Miriam, for you were prepared before your own birth, to receive him. In dream and upon waking you speak with those of the heavens, and, in your birth, were found worthy of carrying the direct descendant of the Annuna. And in their generosity, rather than the fear a single nephalim produced, have delivered two to us."

Miriam studied his face and found no malice in it. For her shame was great that she was not strong enough to carry out the tradition of her people. She had refused to offer up one child in sacrifice before it took breath so that the spirit of the first child would not be broken in half. Instead, she brought him to her breast, while the angels ministered to her needs. Yosef, in turn, because of his love for her, claimed them both as his sons. In that moment, Miriam recalled the morning when they were presented at the Temple.

~~~

Two white doves were found without blemish and as they gave the offering, the priest hesitated until Simeon, the Elder, came forward and took Yeshua unto his arms and said, "Now, I may retire in peace, for as the Sovereign Lord did promise, I see this child will redeem our tribe back into the heavens, and with his light, be the savior of all who see the glory of his radiance." Handing him back to his mother, Simeon took up the second child and spoke, "This is the child of which will befall many sorrows, yet because of him, will we find everlasting joy."

Simeon made the offering to the Lord and recited the prayers. Anna approached them also, and the prophetess touched them both, saying to Yosef, "A child is a gift and these two will double the inheritance. By the grace of God, what was divided becomes greater when two seeds are sown, one upon the earth and the other in heaven."

~~~

Miriam brought her attention back to the man at the table, "What is it that you want from us?"

Melchior's face lit up with a smile that was also seen in his eyes. "My Lady, you have filled our every want and desire. Our caravan has come to offer our small tokens of goodwill. However, on our journey, we were ushered to the house of Herod. In our ignorance, we shared with him the good news. We have been informed by the same holy Grigori that has guided us for these last several months, that Herod, who stated to us his desire to also pay his respects, fears the gift and would seek to destroy you. He sent guards to escort us yet the appearance of the Grigori's speaking star caused them to dispatch. That is why, in our sadness, we have come to seek a private audience without notice of your neighbors. We will not return to Herod."

Zebedee stood and paced as he uttered, "Fear a child! A suckling babe! And to think poor Miriam has beset herself for praising life over following superstitious traditions! We know this Miriam! We know my brother, Yosef! And we know that their union alone was a gift! A priceless contract! And yet you tell us that my brother and this woman are known to you? And that Herod, because your gods found favor in them, would give them to sleep while they nurse?" With an exasperated sigh, Zebedee sat down upon the floor where he stood.

Yosef arose, and placing his hand upon his brother's head to comfort him, spoke gently, "Easy, brother. Our lord will provide." Yosef knew how often, especially in the last years, how miraculously, this was true.

Not two years past, on speculation, Eli-Joachim, to prepare for the wedding of his son, had hired him for a mosaic in their grand hall of his home on the Maath. Everyday Yosef found stone so polished and colorful that he was puzzled with their beauty. Each fit upon the other so perfectly that barely a seam of mortar was applied. When Eli-Joachim and the others of his household came to inspect his work, he asked the most fateful question. "Name your price." Yosef's reward for his skill and his diligent work was worth more than its weight in gold. Yet his love for Miriam had been tested, and here again was proof that God's hand was everywhere they had traveled.

"Tell us, Melchior, what now?" Yosef asked quietly. At that moment, Yosef watched as Yehuda awoke, and taking notice of his surroundings, stretched his arms toward the stranger. Melchior, delighted, extended his long arms and bedecked fingers over the table. Yehuda squealed and took hold of one of the rings on his left hand. Melchior slipped it from his finger and placed it before the child. The ruby encrusted gold flashed in the morning sun. Melchior rose slowly and put the haggard cloak about him.

Motioning to the exquisite ring he said, "Take this as a gesture of my goodwill. I will go and speak with my companions and visit you on the morrow." He raised the hood, and before any could stand, slipped from the courtyard.

The children, who had been quiet the entirety of the visit, became restless and so James and John were sent off with their sisters. Zebedee lifted the ring and measured its heft in his palm. It was impossible for him to conceal his amazement. Zebedee looked to Yosef and asked, "What is it that we will do?"

Without hesitation and noticing the slant now of the sun, Yosef replied, "Keep our appointments." To which he gathered his tools and went off to work.

Late that night, when all were nestled down to sleep, Yosef was awakened by the same messenger whom had guided him before. GabriEl urged, "Yosef, take your family and go with those I have sent you. Go to the lands beyond Egypt where you will be safe until Herod seeks you no longer. Is not your Sovereign Lord the Lord of all?" And the light departed.

Yosef tarried by the door from the moment of dawn.

# ~ Chapter 14 ~

# The Search

*"When Herod realized that he had been outwitted by the Magi, he was furious, and he gave orders to kill all the boys in Bethlehem and its vicinity who were two years old and under, in accordance with the time he had learned from the Magi."*
~ Matthew 2:16

When Yohanan had nearly reached his second birthday, into Jerusalem a great caravan made its way to the palace of Herod. When they did not return with the information for Herod regarding their vision of the King of the Jews, the chief priests consulted for when the child would have been born, and then through determination of the stars and planetary alignments purposed out that the child they sought would be approximately in his nineteenth month. One of the priests who had served in Temple knew of the child born to the old couple of Zecharias and Elsbeth. Considering the high position of Zecharias, it made sense that a male child born after all these barren years could indeed be the miracle that the travelers came to worship.

Herod secretly dispatched a few of his trusted guards to find and to slay the child. Zecharias, as he prepared the incense, was alerted to the presence of the same messenger who had heralded the birth of the son. "Zecharias, take thee son into the deserts. Take thee wife and into the keeping of the Essenes must they go.

Return here to your duties without any eye or ear having awareness of where thy wife and son take refuge." In that hour, Zecharias left the Temple, and going to his wife told of the ominous greeting. In both of their hearts, whatever the reason, they knew without question that they would do this. Gathering only enough for the journey and a few days more, they set off for the closest camp. There Elsbeth and Yohanan were welcomed, and when Zecharias spoke to their High Priests about his vision and the miracle of his son, gladly they received them all into their midst. Zecharias returned before sundown on the following day. Soon after dawn came the Idumaean assassins directly into the Temple. They questioned Zecharias as to the whereabouts of his wife and child, and without hesitation he said, "They sleep in their beds. Why do you trouble an old man and his family who have done nothing?"

The guards simply repeated, "Where is your wife and your son?"

When Zecharias stated he had left them in their beds, the guard snarled while unsheathing his sword, asserting that they had already been there and that no one was at home. Advancing, the guard demanded that Zecharias tell them the whereabouts of the child or forfeit his life. Zecharias answered, "Again, I say to you, I left them asleep in their beds." Raising his weapon above his head in a rage, the leader of the guards swept down his sword which seemed to nearly rip Zecharias in two from his left shoulder to his right hip.

As Zecharias fell to the plinth of the altar, his blood pouring out, a blinding light caused the guards to bring their hands up over their eyes. When their sight was recovered, with the exception of the executioner whose eyes appeared to have been seared from their sockets, all that was found was a smooth red surface between the altar and the door where the body should have lain.

In the desert camp, a ruckus was being made in that same instant. A great light and deafening sound was witnessed as there appeared Zecharias covered in blood, his robe and tunic torn from shoulder to hip. Although no wound was found he remained as if sleeping for several days. Elsbeth continued to bring a cup to his lips and finally, after three days, Zecharias began to swallow heartily. The first question he asked, "The boy?"

# ~ Chapter 15 ~

# Fill the Ewer

*"In the time of Herod king of Judea there was a priest named Zechariah, who belonged to the priestly division of Abijah; his wife Elizabeth was also a descendant of Aaron." ~ Luke 1:5*

Zecharias, who had spent decades preparing the tamid in temple, kicked at the dust as he paced the common courtyard in deep thought. Nothing here to be burned could chase away the demons with sweet enough smoke. He would offer the rarest of resins for his wife - but to enter the town, to show the face of a man presumed dead - he risked the lives of those he loved and those who accepted his teaching in exchange for nourishment and water in this exile. He could only assume his home and his servants, all that he once owned, were now divided. All that he retained was carried in his heart. Elsbeth kept to her chamber in the cave and would take no food. Two days and nights had she rested while her color paled.

Yohanan, who only approached his fifth year, was an enigma to everyone. Perhaps it was the miracle of his birth to his elderly parents which had imparted such wisdom. His comprehension and assessments seemed altogether unsuited for a child. Yohanan tilted his head slightly and looked upon his father's troubled face. "She is not ill, Father. My sister is merely sharing her vigor. Feed Mother from the milk of the ewes and she will rise from her bed by this night."

Zecharias, in swift movement, with eyes stretched wide but not in disbelief, took the shoulders of his son and peered deep into the face of young Yohanan. Zecharias knew that if the quiet boy spoke, with his clipped and precise enunciation, that he had no intention of deception. Yet... a child? Elsbeth was with child? He would have a daughter? The fear and dread was slowly being replaced first with incredulous wonder swiftly followed with incredible joy.

Yohanan showed no response to the actions of his father – unflinching, he looked back upon his father's face with the sincerity of trust. Zecharias did not dispatch the servants but without sound, let go the boy and ran himself to the communal kitchens. He took a full clay pitcher, still warm, and curd, and filled a tray with olives and dried fruit. There, he hurriedly went to his wife, and put the cup to her mouth, and she drank her fill. Soon, she opened her eyes and Zecharias fed her and kept to her side for many days until Elsbeth had her full strength.

Elsbeth named the child Miryam, for Gabriel whispered to both Elsbeth and Zecharias that this child sent to them would also be a handmaid of the Lord, as bright as any star, her light far reaching as a lamp placed upon a high tower. Through her, the Houses of David and of Aaron would be reunited. GabriEl gave instruction that her gender must not keep her from reading or writing, but she was delivered into the care of the learned priest deliberately.

Zecharias included Miryam in all the lessons that he shared with Yohanan and the other children in the camps, and like Yohanan, she studied the text with voracity, and spoke with eloquence of the Law. In the safety of these holy people, Yohanan and Miryam continued to excel and greatly astonished all those who, at first, marginalized the contributions of a child, and especially, of a girl.

# ~ Chapter 16 ~

# Vipers in the Darkness

*"And when thou createst out of the clay, by My leave as the likeness of a bird, and thou breathest into it and it is a bird by my leave." ~ Sura al-Maidah 5:110*

Passing through the edge of the village on their way back to where they were making their new home, they could hear the faintest hissing and mischievous giggles. "Yehuda, it sounds like children playing, why don't we play with them?"

"It's not children we wish to play with, brother. Let us just make our way home." Yeshua always saw the best possibility in every situation. Whether Yehuda's hearing went deeper than Yeshua's, or maybe he was just more on alert after the confrontation at the lakeside, he heard more malcontent than childish laughter, "They're coming… Shh! Quiet! Ready your switches, we'll surprise them around the next corner."

"Slow down, Yeshua, and why don't we take the long way home." Yehuda was trying to avoid the ambush awaiting them down the alley, yet the joy and expectation of making friends moved Yeshua's feet faster than Yehuda had ever seen before.

"Come on, Yehuda! Let's make some friends here in the village!" He quickly turned the corner and Yehuda heard the leaps from the shadows before he could warn his brother. Quickly running after him, he was too late.

Holding Yeshua forcibly by the arms behind his back were the boys from the lakeside. Breathing heavily, and attempting to catch a semblance of composure, Yehuda mustered, "Alright, alright. You have made your point. Let us go and we won't bother you anymore." His hands were on his knees and his back arching with every labored breath. Yeshua was squirming to escape the grasp of his youthfully vile captors. "Seriously, friends, just let my brother go. We haven't done you any harm, and don't wish to cause a scene. Yeshua, just come here."

"You don't order me around, Jew!" The Roman boy came from behind the ones holding Yeshua, out from some dark crevice in the building like a slithering asp. "Why don't we just see how you Jews are accepting of your punishment? We have seen what you and your brother have done to our lands. The spectacle around the waters was interesting for sure. I am surprised that those of your kind didn't punish you harsher."

"What do you know of any of that?" Yehuda seemed surprised and more intrigued that a group of Roman boys would even have any shred of interest in the dealings of "our kind."

"My father knows all that transpires around him. If you had been brought to us…" Pausing for Yeshua and Yehuda to fathom what harsher punishment they would have conceived, "Well, you were not. Either way, this is our land now. If there are to be any adjustments to any of the waterways around here, such as you have done previously, my father would have ordered men to make them. He is quite a smart man, and if there was a need for a hatchery for the fish, he," as if his father was the Lord himself, "would have had it made. Now, if there were some orders you were under from my father to make such a puny lake, I am sure," pure arrogance dripping from the fangs that must be piercing this devil's gums, "he would have you whipped for the disappointing work."

Not wanting to make a scene or cause any harm, Yehuda just wanted to grab Yeshua and get home. They were trying to settle down here, yet these Romans never made it easy for any of them to just live their lives. "You have made your point. Now just let us go on our way home and we will stay away from you forever."

Spreading wide open his arms in disbelief and anger, "I did not say you could speak! We will just add some more to your punishments." Motioning to something behind him, Yehuda suddenly felt his arms being pulled behind my back. Struggling to find freedom would surely make matters worse, yet there was not much he could do.

Even though reason and rationale were rarely the ready implements of the rich and higher classes, their father often found logic to be a tool in dealing with the Romans and other unreasonable men. "What did the lake, that my brother and I built, do to you and your precious settlement? Did the fish do anything to you? I saw no Roman crest upon their scales. We do not wish to eat those fish, so we had no intention of lessening your food supplies. Now you flail willow branches around to taunt some form of punishment on my brother and on me? Surely your father had no intention of giving you any authority over us. We are only children, so just let us go!"

"Enough! My ears bleed from the mere sound of your wretched tongue flapping in the dead air of this dead land we're forced to live in! The only thing I could see worthy of this offence is to have you and your brother whipped with these branches. We will start with this brother you care so much about!" He barked an order to the boys with him, "Hold him to the wall there!"

"You will not!" emphatically leapt from Yehuda's lips and with it the strength of enough men to toss aside the boys holding him back like grains of sand in a storm. Yehuda could hear his voice inside his own head as if someone else was saying the words. "You will release him now. The waters did nothing to you, the fish were not yours, and we will never be yours to command! Now put those switches down and let my brother go!"

In greater shock than if someone had stolen his favorite bag of silver and gold out of his very own hands, the Roman boy faltered at finding a retort. With fear in every word, "What... but... who... I don't..." were the only things he could mutter.

Yehuda stared with such intent at the other older boy holding Yeshua, wanting him to remember this confrontation and their unwavering spirit of determination to not be placed under his Roman thumb. Yehuda commanded him, "Look down at how that willow bough in your hand is all thin and dying. Your own limbs seem to be withering much like the branches you hold. You might just wish to release him and let us go."

Before their eyes, the fingers of the boy began to shrivel and turn white with hairy brown spots appearing on the wrinkled skin. In slow motion, it spread to his arms, as if his body was growing older by the second. He remained the size and stature of a young man, yet his limbs began to haunch and wither, and his words began to shake and stammer, "What is... Someone! Help me!" As he began to look more like a grandfather nearing death, all the boys, including the Roman snake, released them. Quickly they ran from Yehuda sight, whose face resembled a battle plate decorated with burning coals. Yeshua flailed on the ground where he was thrown as Yehuda concentrated on the slow rise and fall of the smithy's bellow in his mind. He must reclaim his regular breathing from that which resembled the huffs of the fabled dragons.

With a sudden calmness and acceptance, almost seeming like nothing had just happened, Yehuda extended a hand to Yeshua to help him up. "Come, Yeshua. We should be getting home." What would they tell Yosef when they got home? Those boys would surely be running to their families to tell them of what they had done - what Yehuda had done.

What had Yehuda done? He said something, and wished it in his heart, and it was simply so. He said it with such deep-felt emotion. Could he have killed that boy? What had Yehuda done?

They walked quite slowly back to the house. Yeshua kept looking at his brother with half wonder and half concern. Yeshua thought to himself, "He never looked afraid, except when that boy had him trapped. Maybe that was what got to him." They took so long to walk; they could have said a prayer for each step they took. Yehuda expressed to Yeshua without looking at him, "Come on, brother, we are only making our punishment worse the longer we take to get home."

"Yehuda," Yeshua pleaded with such adoring love, stopping them at a tree for some rest in the shade, "look at me." He looked into him, and Yeshua looked into his heart. Love pouring from those amber eyes, Yeshua's brow touched Yehuda's and they prayed. Craving the reconciliation of children simply being children with the profound desire for what they all saw happen to that boy to merely be an illusion, they pulled back and simply stared. They knew each would be in one immense pile of trouble when they got home. "Thank you, Yehuda. We must make this right. However, those boys should not be allowed to do what they do. No one who has committed wrong in their life should be able to punish anyone, not even us. We have never harmed another, yet… now… now we must make this right."

# ~ Chapter 17 ~

# Atonement

*"He came to pay a debt He did not owe, because we owed a debt we could not pay." ~ Author Unknown*

They could hear Ima calling from inside the house as Yosef stood in the doorway, hands crossed in front of him, "Barabbas! Would you come here and help me with something? Yosef needs to talk to the boys." Yosef motioned to the grove of trees just east of the house. Some of the most beautiful olive trees were growing that year, yet they doubted their Abba wanted to talk about work or the beauty of the trees.

"How say you about making friends, boys?" Yosef said with such precision. We knew he knew something was not quite right. Part of Yehuda wanted to say, "You already know the answer."

Just as his mouthed opened to answer as his Abba always taught him – to reply with truth and humility the first time when your Father calls you to bring light to his questions – next to him he heard, "Abba. It was I." He looked to Yeshua, and then bowed his head below his shoulders.

Yehuda was as shocked at Yeshua's answer as it seemed Abba was also. The intrigue on Yosef's face was more of a desire to see what direction Yeshua would take with his typically wondrous descriptions. Instead, Yosef asked more directly this time, "It was you? It was you who was about to be beaten by those

Roman boys? Alright, I would accept that as truth. So, Yehuda… what is your half the story?" Yosef had heard many trials in the halls of the Kings for whom he was commissioned to do work. He always wanted to hear the whole story.

"It was me, too, Abba. Yet I think it was me who caused that older boy to wither and almost die. I think I could have killed him. He was about to harm Yeshua, and I am sure the others would have beaten us bloody." Yehuda could have continued into great detail of the scene that had unfolded many hours before. He remembered what Barabbas told him many times, "Boy. It's the simplicity of the facts and the calculated response to the act that one must keep fresh in the mind."

Sighing while considering each of them, and looking through both of them a couple of times, Yosef simply sat back and viewed the stars above them. "Boys…! My boys…! I love you both more than your mother does." A smile crossed his bearded face. "Well, that is probably not even a possibility." Yosef was always able to mix a bit of light-hearted understandings in the midst of great drama or discipline, as these scenarios were typically the boys' case. "In each one of you, whatever it is that you each hold, how does it become something you can use to make this a better world?"

There were many times Yehuda had toyed with Yeshua, making him feel an insect on his ear where none existed. Sometimes he would kiss his Ima on her cheek from across the room. Today, however, something was different. "I tried that today, Abba! Part of me wanted to make all of them go away forever so that our lives could be better without them." A part of Yeshua truly did want to erase their names from the Book of Life. Their lives would be so much better if the Romans were not there to bother them.

A hefty sigh settled upon Yosef's entire being. "Yehuda… Heaven has more in store for each of us than what our minds can even conceive. Better yet, what is inside of you that feels entitled to be the hand of all that is holy?"

Both Yeshua and Yehuda were still caught up in the thought of those boys, yet more specifically Yehuda was stuck on that one Roman tormentor. Just the thought of that viper brought out the same feelings that evoked the battle plate. Yosef knew how to live amongst these "invaders," as Yehuda saw them, and even the greedy of our own people. Yosef was a true holy man in the eyes of the boys and much of their family, as was Barabbas, in his own way. They kept to the holy days and original teachings of the Prophets. Yosef had the same peace about him as Yeshua. It was an acceptance of their place in the scheme life. All Yehuda could muster was humbly, "Yes, Abba."

Pulling closer to Yehuda, he placed a single finger under his chin, and drew his head up. Yehuda surely thought this grasp was about to deliver some profound statement mixed with another punishment. Yet it came with no verbal lashing, just love pouring from those dark eyes they shared. Those deep feeling eyes rushed Yehuda close, embracing him with such concern and affection mixed together. "Yehuda, Yehuda… Oh, Yehuda. You and Yeshua have such great gifts of love and life. The dreams brought to me by the angels of the Lord… Yehuda, Yehuda…"

Yehuda pulled away from him, even though he always enjoyed being close to Abba. Yeshua was truly Miriam's boy, and Abba and Yehuda were the closest most times. As a boy will always jump to his Ima when the moment demands it, it was Yosef and Yehuda… They had no way to convey their understanding, just that he and his Abba just understood each other.

"Yosef?" The call came from the inner recesses of the house with the upward tonal clarity only Miriam could muster. "Yosef? You and the boys have to go into town and clear this up. Immediately!"

Yosef pulled Yeshua over to them from his praying beneath the olive tree. Yosef had a coy smile on his face as if to secretly say something to Miriam in his head that brought him ease before the coming storm in town. "Let's go, boys. The parents of those other boys want your heads on a platter. They surely want to know how and why the one has withered to a ripe old age to rival his grandfather. Do either one of you have an explanation for that?"

"He deserves it." If he had been a little quicker with his tongue, Yehuda would have begun to postulate an excuse, yet it was Yeshua who bleated that out. Yehuda could only agree with a tilt of his head as he looked up at Yosef's raised eyebrows. It was as if they glanced at each other in the amazement of Yeshua's response.

As Yosef's chest expanded with enough air to begin a long diatribe of acceptances, postulations and approaches on how to deal with what chaos awaited, he simply alleged, "Well… that may be. Just put your life in the hands of the Almighty and let him guide you."

The walk into town was long enough to think and pray for wisdom and peacefulness. Yehuda kept thinking that surely the Roman boy would be there. If he was any more a product of his father as they were of Yosef's demeanor, the impending confrontation could be the beginning of a battle. Stares... how Yehuda despised staring. The entire toe-to-toe exchange a stare painted in the mind. He considered how he would much prefer to just get it over with rather than playing stupid games.

Abba paused at the door to a quite opulent home. Many inscriptions surrounded the elaborate tile work that Abba admired. This must be the snake's home. Of course, his father would be someone affluent enough to equal his son's ego, and it was an obvious show of strength to bring them all here. We could hear the foreign tongues shouting back and forth, surely offering our exit from either this town or this world. The smell of doom had a pungent and sulfuric odor, or that just might be the spices these Romans stole from the last land they conquered.

As if they heard the thoughts on his mind, or simply the dread on his face, both Yeshua and Yosef looked Yehuda's way, yet it was Yeshua who said, "In His hands, brother. In His hands, we always are."

They all took the deepest of breaths as the heavy double doors groaned open painfully. Yehuda noticed the gears of Abba's mind turn to look and inspect with precision the heavy doors and the weighted mechanisms just inside. Yosef pulled Yeshua and Yehuda behind him as he questioned the man who greeted them. Yosef pointed to the weights and pulleys. The man contemplated his directions with understanding and intrigue. He only answered Yosef with a nod. The door man pointed to the courtyard further down into this palatial home, and then continued looking back at the mechanisms that made the door swing. Yehuda, too, was intrigued, and could have stood there like the sentry at the door, yet Yosef pulled the boys to continue on to their trial.

The accusations and leering gazes were met with pointed fingers and waving, dismissing gestures of all the parents and children gathered. What would become of them? What had Yehuda done to his family? The thought entered his mind that surely they would be asked to move on or perhaps a more severe punishment would be decreed. Hearing Yehuda's thoughts as usual, "Brother, it will be as it is. In His hands, brother," Yeshua whispered behind Yosef's back as they neared the Roman boy and his judgmental father. As they approached, a tall, dark-haired, slender man rose from an ornate chair with the command of one of their own Senators. He even looked as politicians had been described to the boys by the others in town. The whitest of robes encircling his wiry frame, he had the same dark gem pendant hanging from his neck that the vile snake of a child flaunted everywhere he went. It was as if he was advertising his authority over the world as he encountered it.

Booming throughout the room, "We have all come here to hear the contrived words of a couple boys, if they have any semblance of an ability to defend themselves. Out of courtesy to these people forced to be our neighbors in this… heartbroken land, I have called for your high priests to insure proper judgment as our laws have yet to be accepted by… your people…in these matters." His son surely acquired the sting of his father's diction, yet this man at least had some degree of restraint that his son had yet to even conceive.

Yehuda tugged on father's robes, "Abba, let us just give him what every Roman desires. We have plenty of it and have never truly wanted or had any need for it. What is a sack of shiny metal to us?"

Ignoring Yehuda with everything in a dismissive glance, Yosef said proudly, "These are my sons. I have claimed them from their birth. Neither of them would harm a hair on the leg of a gnat lest they be harmed in some fashion. There must have been some reason for these boys to have retaliated in any way against such noble boys of the Roman caste. We all know boys will be boys and often the ones in the wrong will often go to great lengths to cast doubt and suspicion on anyone they might. I have…"

Interruption was common with the Roman people that had become their "friends" at the end of a sword. "Are you claiming any sense of superiority over a Roman, Galilean? I have traveled from the forests of the Aquitania to the encroaching deserts of Numidia, and I have yet to be treated as such from the likes of the Jewish people of Judaea! Your station amongst these cities here in…" Interruption from his own people, however, seemed to cause him great distress as one of his servants, the same one who opened the large doors for them, caught his ear with a whisper. The words were inaudible from even the boy's highly adept senses.

Uncle Barabbas had trained them to sit for hours listening first to this bug, then this beast and that winged creature. Yeshua would often talk to a cloud of gnats, asking them to bother anyone else but them, and they would merely fly off as if commanded by his kind words.

This aide or servant, who spoke to this stately Roman judge, was motioning to the creaking door where they had entered. All they could hear of this conversation was, "...He carries the seal of which King?"

"...their only accomplished King since the fabled King David who slew the Giant of Gath... from Herod the Great... Suppose this Jew could lend aid to the failings of our own architects? His understandings of engineering and architecture surely make this family one unworthy of your heel... Sir." Although this aide or servant, or whatever his station to garner such consideration, only briefly diverted attention away from the boys, the inner conflict being raised within the mind of this Roman statesman seemed to be claiming victory over the whining of his evil son.

"Yosef, your talent is well known throughout this region, and I am informed many of my fellow Romans know your skill as well."

It did seem everyone here acknowledged Yosef for who he was as a skilled tekton, but more than a common laborer, as a fine artisan and somewhat of an architect or engineer. After contemplating and weighing the elements of the decision he was about to hand down, he motioned to his son, "Listen to your father, boy. Is what you have told us about your friend true?" The statesman had refused to examine the child who could have any sort of contagious disease and instead ordered him to be covered in layers like the unclean lepers, forcing him to remain in the corner alone. "Before you answer me hastily," stopping his son from making any mistake even he could not redeem, "be sure you know which boy it is here that stands before me. Their father is a man who carries the seal of their former King Herod. Do you remember what the Kings of this land have done for Rome?"

Devoutly demure as a sucking child, he glared at Yeshua and Yehuda, and strained his eyes to catch a closer focus on our faces. "Abba, do you see how he looks at us? He cannot see us well at our distance. Move us back a few steps," Yehuda whispered, knowing the poor sight was a product of his Roman breeding.

Seeing as they did, with great precision and clarity as true artisans to pay attention to detail, "Honorable statesman of Rome, it is true that I bear with me the Seal of King Herod the Great, yet no special treatment do I claim it to hold for me." Recognizing a stream of sunlight coming through the ornate ceiling Yosef had been analyzing since they arrived, he stepped them back, raising his hand that carried the Seal of Herod, "and perhaps a greater light shall shine on the matter your son strains to see." Selecting the words his father would recognize to the illumination of his son's visual lack, Yosef tempered this man's impending judgment.

The statesman's head tilted back to a glare across the bridge of his nose, glanced over to his son still straining to see what Yosef was holding and also struggling to differentiate between Yeshua and Yehuda who clung to the shadows of Abba's robes, he breathed a sigh of impending defeat. "It is obvious to those who can see," and as snidely as his contrived posture could convey, "we are at an impasse of understanding the transgressions of a group of young boys gathering the hubris of their youth to claim their superiority over one another. I propose that…"

As he droned on and on with words that began to climb heights even the Romans could not comprehend, Yeshua seemed to be staring at the withered boy in the corner of the room. He began to utter words of which Yehuda only understood a portion. The soft voice reminded him of the holy men from the caves in the hills that Barabbas visited. Something within Yehuda understood that the same power and control over the reality around us was coming to a head as it did at the former Lake Yeshua.

"Hear my words, Abba, and know my name as your son. Return this boy to his former self, for he knows not what truths lay within his soul. He shall be loved by your beloved and know your heart as I know it to be. My brother commanded his punishment for the safety of our family. Return this boy to his former self now, less a small reminder of his transgression."

Sitting back on his throne, the Roman statesman continued, "Bring your sons closer so that we may entertain what possibility of punishment shall be levied upon their heads."

Pushing his own son behind his seat, he motioned for them to come closer. "Also, bring forth the boy who has been afflicted by the alleged wickedness of these two boys."

The boy came from the corner as he was ordered under the shaking of a heavy hooded robe to hide his shame. "Boy! Show us your body so withered by the magical workings of these Jewish mystics standing before us."

From underneath his hood, he glowered through his cowl, and with a fling of superiority and a pull of his cloak, the robes fell to the ground leaving him as bare as his mother first saw him. With a myriad of giggles and snickers echoing in the courtyard, standing with legs spread wide and arms open, expecting to show the evil they had caused him, his skin instead shined as white as the alabaster stones of the Temples of Jerusalem. Yehuda tugged at Yosef to whisper in his ear, "Not one single piece of him is as withered as I had made him!"

Amidst the gasps and giggles abounding the courtyard, Yosef pushed Yehuda behind him again. The Roman statesman frowned deeply from his raised throne and shot out of his seat, casting his own indigo shawl from his shoulders to cover the naked boy. "Cover yourself and embarrass Rome no more!"

Leaning closer so that not everyone in the hall could hear him, he made clear his disappointment, "How dare you cast your inequities of your family before this gathering?" Truly was he just as he had originally been, except for one diminutive member which might cause him some ridicule in his later years.

Yehuda looked over to his brother smiling behind Yosef's robes, looking for acknowledgement from him. Casting Yeshua a wink of approval of this boy's now waning ability to carry on his family's line, he knew they would be returning home with little worry of any more issue from these children or their families.

The vile Roman boy looked on in amazement as his friend hurriedly covered his naked exposure. His glance shot their way as to ask what they did to clear the "curse" he reported to his father.  Yehuda's reply was a simple shrug.

From behind Yosef came Yeshua, standing with the same regality as the Roman statesman had when we entered, touting with authority, "I am sure that our families can prosper together in this land you curse yet one that we call home.  This land has much to share with those who inhabit it, if they treat her with respect.  I cast no ill upon any of those boys, wishing merely to foster a home for fish in a pool separate from the river.  They chose to cast their intentions upon our deeds and upon our namesake.  Surely in your laws, as is in ours, are ways to handle such ill intended reprisals?"

Amazed as all were at the diction and understanding of decorum amidst these foreign statesmen, the Roman answered, "Certainly, we do, young man.  Know that these children," again a snide comment across the bridge of that distinct nasal feature, "shall not bother the like of your kin or kind ever again, as long as they hold residence within my home and jurisdiction.  Who are you, young man?"

Looking back at Yosef, Yeshua sought approval from him to answer truthfully.  Gaining the nod of approval from him, Yeshua motioned to his brother to stand with him, and with trepidation mixed with trust in his brother's ability to conjure peace in the toughest of crowds, they boldly stepped forward.  "We are Yeshua and Yehuda bar Yosef, and descendants of David by both our Mother Miriam and Father Yosef, princes in the line of the true Kings of this land, and children of the one true Lord.  Even though some of your growing sons may harbor our property in their hilt, we stand before you not needing such opulence to hold true to our lineage. Our Kingdom comes on the wings of eagles and the breath of the Creator who generated your name before you broke the door of life into this world. We bid you to leave us to our lives as we see fit. Thank you, sir. We will be leaving now."

Taking each a hand of Yosef as they stepped back, the Roman elder quietly said with peace on his heart, "Well, then Sons of David. You have made your father and mother proud this day. Surely Roman children could learn a few lessons from you and your brother. Inside my heart warms an understanding that this is not the last we will see of each other. Gaius!" motioning to his son behind him, "Bid these Sons of Kings their good tidings and assurances you will not have any further dealings with them such as today."

Yehuda's words not having an audible tongue, "Gaius, is it? Gaius, I will remember you. As the blade of King David swings at your hilt, my mind will forever know you. Remember these faces, Gaius. You will see me again. As the Lord carries my name, I will carry yours on my heart forever and more."

As his eyes crept across the floor as the snake that entwined his heart, the blackness of his eyes glared into Yehuda with further curses unutterable, "Most assuredly... Father," as a gentle reminder to the back of his skull came from his father's hand, "Father! I understand! I will not bother these boys ever again, I swear it!"

"Then that is the end of it. Before you leave us, Yosef?" Gaius' father motioned Yosef over to where he stood. "I understand you have a great knowing of the machinations of our Roman architecture and engineering. I would like to have a word with you after everyone departs." To all who had gathered, "Go to your homes as this matter is ended. Go about your days!" Yosef was shown the way to a more private area to converse with him further, "Yosef? With me if you would." They both headed toward the doorway with the aide who welcomed them.

Yosef hurried his boys along, "Go home to your mother and assure her all is well. She will be concerned and undoubtedly praying in the courtyard. Go to her and tell her I am arranging further work for our family." They ran from the courtyard and all the way home.

~~~

As they approached the grove of olives, just as Yosef had mentioned, they found Miriam praying with tears in her eyes. When Yeshua took the announcement from Yehuda's lips, she leapt with joy, "Praise be to the Lord as he has delivered you back into my arms, my precious boys! Praise be to the Lord!"

"It was simple mother," Yeshua peddled. "All is well now, and the Romans have sworn never to bother our family again. I told them who we were and the Roman statesman is now working out a contract with Yosef."

"Abba," Yehuda asserting his proper title, and again reminding his brother of the respect any son should show, "is working out some sort of work on their opulent home, Ima."

Either way, he was right. The Romans should not bother them again, yet he knew this would not be the last they saw of Gaius.

# ~ Chapter 18 ~

# The Temple

*"He said to them, "Why were you looking for me? Do you not know that it was fitting for me to be in my Father's house?" ~ Luke 2:49*

"Yosef," Miriam rushed to her husband, "Yeshua is nowhere to be found. We are in the city during the busiest time of the year and I fear for his safety." The worry and harried excitement took over every part of Miriam. Her son, the boy she had kept safe for all these years was out of her reach and knowing of his safety.

Yosef was always calm even in the worst of situations, and the loss of his young son could be the worst he had seen in years since their exodus to Egypt. Attempting to assuage his young wife's fears, he knew if they found his brother, Yeshua could not be far behind. Miriam looked at him in his silence looking for answers, "Where is Yehuda? Surely, he knows where Yeshua is, and is probably with him also."

Yosef may have been calm in demeanor, yet his mind was racing through the worst scenarios. Suddenly an answer or at least a direction came to him, "Last I saw Yehuda, he and Barabbas were speaking with friends of Barabbas'. I will find him!"

Miriam paced back and forth, now and then slapping Yosef's arm in her fears, she came upon a hope. "Why are you not going? I'm going with you!"

Already heading toward the city from where they had camped, he shouted to her, "If that is your wish, come!"

They had climbed this rise and that fall in the city streets. They grabbed at many who could have been Barabbas, some who could have been either Yehuda or even Yeshua. Finally Yosef spotted Barabbas and Miriam rushed to him, "Barabbas! Have you seen Yehuda? Last we saw him…"

Barabbas pointed to the knife salesman down the way, "He is enthralled with the knives and blades over there."

Miriam ran quicker than the wind to her son and knelt down to him and looked up into his eyes, holding his hands in her own, "Yehuda! Where is your brother? He is not where he should be," and standing to solidify her disappointment she admonished Yehuda with her motherly softness, "and for that fact, neither are you."

He looked at her with fear and guilt, and slowly tears began to well in his eyes. He looked to Yosef who stood behind Miriam. "Sorry, Abba."

With a heavy sigh and a paternal hand on his wife's shoulder, he looked at his son and tried to calm the guilt storming up in his face. "Yehuda. It's alright, we just need you to remember where Yeshua is. Your Ima fears for his safety, and if you are not with him…" Yosef placed a hand on Miriam and on Yehuda. His calm could at times be transferred with a mere touch.

Choking back his own concern, Yehuda came to an epiphany, "Yeshua is probably listening to the priests near the Temple! I can show you where he has been going since we arrived here in the city."

Miriam excited at a direction, and Yosef finding pride in his son, yet it was Miriam in her determination, "Yes! Take us right away!"

"We have been meeting here by the stairway of the Temple." Looking around nervously as Yeshua was diligent in meeting up with his brother. "He should be here by now. I was late meeting up with him." Yehuda was typically the one who was admonished for not arriving at the rendezvous.

Seeing his nervousness, Yosef calmed his son's concern with a simple pat on the shoulder. "We will talk about that later, Yehuda. We must find Yeshua before your mother loses her senses."

As they approached the Temple steps, there was a crowd of priests discussing something important and a crowd of onlookers began to form at the doors to the Temple. Yehuda pointed to the crowd, "Up there, Abba? There is a crowd of priests up there inside the Temple. I can see them in the doorway. Where there is a crowd of people, Yeshua is typically there."

Passing through Yosef and Yehuda, Miriam rushed up the stairs, "Yeshua! Yeshua!" She continued to call Yeshua as they ran up the stairway behind her.

Miriam and Yosef were searching through the crowd as Yehuda exclaimed, "Abba! I hear him! He is talking with the priests."

From within the crowd of priests you could hear many questioning, "How do you know such things, young one?" Some were wrought with emotion at something that had been said, "Get him out of this temple!" Some of the chief priests had heard enough and were calling for action, "Call the guards!"

Yosef made his way through the priests as respectfully as he could, grabbing Yeshua by his arm, "Yeshua, come with us. Stop bothering these men."

As he collected Yeshua and began to usher him past the priests who wanted this boy taken into custody, Yosef played again the part of the peacemaker in the family. "My apologies for my son's annoyances."

One of the priests, who seemed to know Yosef, came to their side. He was a round and robust man in his later years yet still young enough to live a life well enough to insulate him from the cold nights. He didn't seem as bothered by what Yeshua had been saying, yet seemed more concerned about his safety and exodus from his vindictive brethren

"I am Nicodemus. It would be wise of you to exit the Temple as soon as you can before their ire brings them to holding your son for further questioning. Some wish to bring him to the Sanhedrin, and that is a destination your wife would not care for her son." His concern was growing as he looked back over their shoulders. He was hurriedly, yet covertly ushering the family out of the Temple and back into the streets.

Nicodemus looked for an inconspicuous spot to continue discussing what had happened only moments before. Finding an area just around the eastern side of the Temple, he brought the family into the alley. While fear was his initial demeanor, it was intrigue and a desire to know more that directed him in his mission of secrecy.

He looked at Yosef and then at Miriam, yet spoke directly to Yosef, "We must speak with you and your wife about this boy, if he is claimed by you."

Yosef stood proud and somewhat indignant at the thought of both of his boys being questioned of their heritage. Yehuda seemed to identify a hint of concern at the question evident in the shifting of Yosef's eyes. Still Yosef said with conviction, "He is mine as I have claimed him at his birth."

Nicodemus continued, "What is his name? He has understandings and a knowing that no boy his age should have. He confuses even the greatest of our Rabbis."

He clapped a hand on Yeshua's shoulder with pride and declared, "His name is Yeshua." Without hesitation nor a sense of delay, his other hand clapped the shoulder of Yehuda, "This is his brother Yehuda."

Nicodemus bent down slightly, grabbing Yeshua by the jaw with Yeshua's chin raised, cheeks pressed in to almost create a pucker on his lips. He somewhat forcefully turned and examined every inch of Yeshua's face. He did the same to examine Yehuda, looking back at Yeshua, then back to Yehuda, back to one then the other again. Standing from his physical examination of the boys, he looked around Yosef's face, back to the boys and back to Yosef. With raised eyebrows, as if to understand that there seemed to be some incongruity in the claim that Yosef had made, Nicodemus grabbed his robes as if he were to suddenly pass judgment.

"The similarity in their faces, especially of their eyes, is quite intriguing. While we have seen the one called Yeshua on a number of occasions, the other one is presumed to be the cloaked one Yeshua meets up with after leaving the Temple." Nicodemus looked down at the boys with a raised brow. After the tiniest of reaction, he winked at Yehuda.

"Which one of these is the first and which of them is the last? The reason that Yehuda is the shrouded boy Yeshua meets with daily at the end of our lessons is now evident."

Yosef answered with the art of a Roman orator or even one of the guile-filled Sanhedrin, "They are both my sons, equal in most respects with their own unique and differing qualities."

Yosef, understanding the implications which Nicodemus insinuated, reached for his sons, who did not pull away. "This," he intoned as he held Yeshua close to him saying, "is the first born, the one who will redeem Israel from destruction. And this," holding Yehuda even closer to him, claimed, "is Yehuda. I have declared him also as mine own. He, too, will watch over the children of Israel. I have claimed them both."

There was no fear in Yosef's demeanor nor his eyes, which Nicodemus was intently studying for some hint of deception. With the words Yosef uttered as if professed by the angels, Nicodemus' concern and questioning melted into the round and pleasant figure he was inside.

The joy of the declaration rang through his heart and soul, and became a changed man in that moment. "Salvation is what he will need if the instruction he desires to give continues to be uttered in the Temple. Many of my brothers are intrigued as to what your son has to speak of, yet it scares all of us to the point of claiming a worse crime than any of us here would care to entertain."

Directing Yeshua toward Miriam and silently imploring Miriam to make her way back to camp, "Yeshua, go to your mother."

Thanking Nicodemus for the generosity of his rescue of Yeshua from the priests of the Temple, Yosef and Yehuda pardoned themselves. "We will be on our way, and please pardon our son for bothering you and all within these holy walls."

Nicodemus glanced around him and pulled Yosef and Yehuda to a shadowy spot unseen from the walls of the Temple. "Listen to me, for this must be understood. Your son, Yosef, has brought a great deal of attention to himself. The knowledge he has," as he looked toward the heavens, "he should not have. However miraculous I may recognize his gift of the understanding of creation and the Law as it was given to the first of all of us, this does not matter to the rest of the Council. He has drawn attention to himself and this is attention that you do not want. Where is it that you come from during these holy days?"

The grasp Nicodemus had on Yosef's arm surely conveyed the severity of a warning that he was trying to convey. Worry began to enter into Yosef's face as he responded, "We have made a home for ourselves in the region of Galilee."

Nicodemus was a Pharisee and could not give specific direction for the family to take, yet he felt he must warn them of the future that lay ahead of them. "All I can tell you, my friend, is that the eyes and ears of the Sanhedrin span a great distance and they will surely have their attention directed your way. This attention will assuredly follow you for quite some time."

# ~ Chapter 19~

# The Eyes

*"His eyes are like doves by the water streams, washed in milk, mounted like jewels." ~ Song of Solomon 5:13*

Miryam remembered the first time she saw his eyes – Yehuda's golden flecked eyes she could see from such a distance– something like the feral cats as he observed those around him yet kept himself aloof, his face pointed as if he had chewed something sour. And then, how she had scrubbed her eyes with her fists as if her vision had played tricks for another boy just like him was seen in the midst of the newcomers, already her frail mother greeting a woman and these boys in the valley. She nearly forgot to stir the pot when her brother came to stand beside her.

"Yohanan, why do they come? Do we know them?" She shifted her gaze to the pot and to the fire and then down upon her brother's dusty feet. She could feel him keeping his emotions in check. Always cautious, always concerned with who might come this way, she felt in Yohanan a different reaction – was it fear? Why did her brother's heart race as quickly as hers? Who might they be? She knew now that Yohanan recognized these people, these strangers wandering out to their desert home.

Looking into her brother's face and grasping at his arm, she implored, "Yohanan, tell me who they are?" He said nothing in reply while he gently removed her hand from his sleeve and brushed past her. He felt her eyes on his back as he descended the slope from the mouth of the cave to the windswept path below.

Miryam could see the stranger woman and her mother Elsbeth had ended their deep embrace yet still clung to one another's arm. A man stood behind this woman, all smiles, as it seemed the stranger's children were presented to her mother, young boys and girls who danced about kicking up dust as they were embraced one by one. Miryam was frustrated that she could observe yet the winds took away the sounds, the voices, of this meeting. The two older boys came next and Miryam was shaken to see her mother sway for a moment. Her mother was much older than the common mother here, but of course, Miryam had not seen much of the world. As her mother stumbled, one of the boys caught her elbow and easily steadied her. It was at that moment that Yohanan arrived, clasping Mother's shoulders.

The next moment, Miryam saw a strange thing as Yohanan went to one knee before this woman but ever so quickly, the woman, kissing his cheek, pulled him to standing and embraced him with great vigor. Then the older boys each clapped a hand to Yohanan's shoulders, heads nodding as they spoke to one another. Standing there with the other boys, Yohanan, with his hair blowing all about his face as always, was a head taller and much broader yet they seemed about the same age. While Miryam was still figuring out what all this embracing of strangers could mean, she realized that her mother had gestured her way and now, just now, all eyes were fixed on her.

Dropping the spoon, she entered the cave calling, "Father, Father!"

"Miryam! Zecharias!" The stranger woman was now with Mother at the cave. As Miryam helped her father to his feet, he began to cry out her name but looked past her. It took his daughter a moment to realize that he called to the woman standing there and Miryam, in all the confusion, began to laugh. She laughed in such a manner that her Father questioned if she had taken ill which in turn caused her to laugh more deeply at his furrowed face.

"No, Father, no! I am well! I am well! There is something within me that sings with joy and I cannot contain it!"

It seemed, however, to be contagious as the stranger with her same name began to laugh until tears ran down her face. "Come child, let me see you!"

~~~

In the weeks to come, these two shared much laughter and many tears. Miryam leaned against Miriam as Zecharias placed the last of the white stones upon the mound. Elsbeth had passed on holding both their hands just as the dawn cleared the shadows of the night. In her last motion, Elsbeth had placed her daughter's hand into the hand of her kinswoman. And now, Miriam held Miryam close as her cousin, her friend, and her confidant was returned to the dust.

Yehuda, Yeshua, and Yosef stood silently. Arms limp at his sides, Yeshua opened and closed his fists repeatedly as he watched the two women – the two women that he loved. Yes, he knew in his heart that

Miryam, with the fire in her hair and the sea in her eyes, was the only woman with whom he could ever imagine walking the lonely road ahead of him. How he wanted to ease her pain, to yell at the earth to release her mother! And yet, what good would it be now? Death would keep coming.

All alone, Yohanan stared into the sky.

~~~

Zecharias called down to Miryam while she did the washing in the small pool. "Yes, Father! Yes!" For all her knowledge, and all her wisdom, her youthful joy carried away the appearance of her astute ability to discuss and debate with even the Nazerene order of priests here among this camp of Essenes. Zecharias shook his head at her exuberance as she bounded to his feet.

"Daughter, I have something I wish to ask you…" but Miryam interrupted him, "Yes, Father, I have already answered you!" All Zechariah could do was to continue to shake his head.

Lifting her chin and looking into the sea, he amusingly chastised her, "I waited decades for children. Do not keep an old man from his grandchildren!"

# ~ Chapter 20 ~

# Stop Them!

*"And Yeshua entered The Temple of God and he began to cast out those who bought and sold in The Temple and he overturned the tables of the money exchangers and the seats of those who were selling doves." ~ Mark 11:15*

The sun beat down harshly while the clamoring of hoof step and bridled whickering snorts echoed the demand for order and compliance in the distance. "Where are your elders? Your priests! Do they abandon you now?" came with such contrite and demeaning thunder. The clanking of their armor, the clang of their swords on their shields as they attempted to make their supreme presence known grated the ears of all who were simply milling about their days.

"We have the highest of orders to bring the rebels to the Governor. You have until the sun crests the sky. All of them, no matter their age or status amongst your wretched gatherings you call family, are to be handed over! Let the Gods sort them. Yes, Judea," he hissed atop such a marvelous steed, "we are your Roman Masters, and you WILL do as you are told!" Only the Romans were allowed to ride such gracious animals. Fury filled their immense eyes as they were poked and prodded by some of the vilest beasts in all of creation.

A band of agitators had broken into the tax collector's villa. The soldiers had been dispatched to retrieve the stolen property and the guilty parties. The description was simply youthful Jewish males. To the soldiers, any boy that was caught would be punished. Everyone knew how.

"Yehuda, we must run to find Father! We must tell him! We must go back to the Temples in the South where the fathers of Moses have surely forgotten us! Brother!" Yehuda would pay no heed to his pleas to run away.

"Why are you constantly choosing to run away to avoid any confrontation? I am always the one having to keep you safe. Stay where you are, Yeshua."

In confusion, Yehuda's younger brother Joses, eyed him warily.

A young soldier clamored down the alley on a young black stallion following behind an older, more polished and worn soldier of the Emperor. The Emperor's Guard was in their village. Surely there was a more significant reason why they had been sent into the region.

As the young soldier passed, a glimmer from the blade in the soldier's boot caught his eye. The mark on its hilt looked somewhat familiar. Where did a Roman soldier get that blade?

In a moment of clarity amidst the commotion, Yehuda recalled when he last saw that blade, and the memory became a vivid recollection amidst this chaos.

Back down in the square were shouts and cries of the women who wanted nothing of this latest edict. "We must run away," is all Yehuda heard since they were born. Yet Kings ran toward them, bringing them their richest of herbs and oils and metals. Offering them finely wrought caskets to hold their life's worth of wealth. Beaded and tasseled robes to clothe the most revered priests were laid before their feet. Simple people are we? Yehuda's thoughts were loud enough for the trained ear to hear, "One day, even the highest and mightiest of Romans will bow to my brother and I. We are the Princes of David, heathen thugs! Spit on your own mothers graves before you defile our presence!" Sometimes thoughts escape the lips of eager teenage boys easier than grains of sand through the hand.

"Brother! Keep quiet!" Joses hushed, trying not to give up his location. Always keeping quiet is how they survived. It was what Barabbas had taught them. Although Barabbas said it was all they needed to really know, Yeshua had taught Yehuda things in the garden while Miriam and Yosef, and many of the family who would gather from time to time, would be amazed at his understandings. Boys older than them had yet to learn most things Yeshua knew of the world even if they found a Master to teach them. Miriam often said Yeshua was the "Master who will teach." Yet, Yehuda often wondered, as most teenage children do, who he truly was. Yehuda acted as the watcher, the keeper, the errand boy of the brother Miriam told the other adults was "he who is to save us all." Yehuda's thoughts often proclaimed, "What of my dreams, my understandings and my knowing?" If he spoke while he dreamed, as Yeshua often did, some would be even more concerned for his mental stability.

Miriam had also called him "The Redeemer," "the fulfiller of all written prophecy." Yosef always called him as he saw him – Hebrakah, or blessing, in their native tongue. Yosef accepted, yet Yehuda felt that his Ima knew more. Yehuda had a great knowing as well, and he saw a great deal more than others did. Both of their senses were heightened, yet Yehuda seemed to have a greater range of senses. Even though the staring by others troubled Yeshua, it brought a heavier concern to Yehuda. He could often see eyes glaring at him from the hidden paces. He could hear the chilling laughter in the empty spaces as they passed between villages. How could they know, see, and hear so well, so similarly and yet Yeshua seemed to be able to control it better? Perhaps it was because he came first into the world and received most of the gifts of life; and now Yeshua was too involved with that woman and his own physical pleasures to even notice Yehuda's torments. Maybe it was because Yehuda came too late to receive the blessing of the Lord. Could he be cursed? This thought too often ran wildly through his mind.

Yehuda, without a concern for safety or danger, with great determination, replied, "Leave me and run, brother! I have swung heavier a sword in many other times!" He pushed him back to the alley with a mere movement of his hand. With the same serenity and calmness Yeshua often carried with him on his robes, Yehuda snarled, "he is no threat to me!" This young soldier might have seen many Jews in his time, and had probably notched his steed's bridle more than anyone cared to know. Yehuda would not forgive him this time. "I will not run again!"

Melding Yehuda's memories with reality, the dark shadows where he had flung Joses to save him, whispered, "Mother will have our hides! Come now!"

"Save him at all costs!" his Ima constantly told him when they wandered into town. A mother commands, and her son obeys. Yet the clouds of his own darkness shrouded Yehuda that this was Joses, not Yeshua.

They could hear the announcement of their location from scout to sentry and all down the line of the Roman barbarians. "Over here are two of them! They look young enough to be the ones we are looking for!" Joses ran with all his might not only to escape but to also find help. The young soldier spun his horse in their direction. The hooves of this once gentle mount, now turned to a war machine by the brutality of his master, turned skillfully in an instant and stared Yehuda down as he stood in the middle of the street.

"Why, look what I have found. A fighting Jew! Wait. Could it be? Why, yes it is. It is you, isn't it, Yehuda bar Yosef?" Pulling the curved blade from his boot straps, the dark jewel glinting in the noon sun, he rolled it and fanned it with toying delight. The mark of the Kingdom of David was the only thing Yehuda's eye kept in view. "Recognize this, Jew?"

The soldier looked at Yehuda as he stared at the blade. Turning his horse to confront him, "What is it you stare at? This is my father's knife, stupid Jew! It was a gift to his eldest."

"Of course, Roman viper, that's me, the stupid Jew! We get jeweled blades for our celebrations of life, while you get to eat one more day from the spoils of your expeditions to foreign lands," Yehuda retorted. Yeshua would have pitied that young man's soul, yet pity was not even a glimmer in Yehuda's heart.

"And that's because we bring you the opulent grace of the Gods to this forsaken wasteland. Jews! What a waste of resources. At least I will put good use to this supposed holy blade of some grubby priest. Maybe you would like to see it closer, Jew?"

Stealing and claiming ownership seemed the prime directive of every Roman Yehuda had met. How ironic that they searched for the rightful owners of the coinage ripped from starving households.

"That blade has the mark of King David on it. That blade belongs to my family! By the grace of the Almighty Creator..." The rush of people interrupted Yehuda's desires to charge into that Roman boy, now grown, from those earlier encounters in the alley and the lakes he and Yeshua created – the Roman statesman's son, Gaius.

"We are here to round up all guilty Jews. All those about your age, Yehuda! Any uprising has been ordered to be put down, and you and your brother will be my shining glory today! Where is he? You two are never far from each other." He looked around, peering through the windows, down the alleyways. "I remember what you and he did to us back then. That, I will never forget, desert devil! Come out here and save your brother again, why don't you?"

Repeating himself, "That is a ceremonial blade of the House of David, Roman," Yehuda hissed. Horses have an instinctual fear of snakes, and how that noble animal allowed a viper to be his master was unknown to Yehuda, yet perhaps it was his declaration on fiery breath that caused the reaction that ensued. Gaius' trusty steed reared and threw its rider with vengeance. The people around them laughed at this display, and even harder at the cloud of dust surrounding the dismounted Gaius. Even his comrades found it humorous. "His horse is afraid of a Jew!" they touted with hearty laughter. Yehuda found his inept attempt to stay saddled quite amusing as a toothy sneer partnered with his steady glare.

Enraged, Gaius taunted, "Then why don't you come and get it!" as he tossed the blade back and forth from hand to hand.

"It's been defiled for much too long. I have many other riches at my command. More than you will ever know. It's time you left us now." If Yehuda were to confront this bully now, it would need to be for the last time.

Yehuda lunged toward Gaius, pinning the wrist holding the dagger to the ground. Yehuda sneered at Gaius, "I will disarm you, if it's the last thing I do, and reclaim our inheritance to the throne."

Gaius spit directly into Yehuda's face, yet the simple secretions were like venom in Yehuda's eyes. In that moment Gaius twisted and claimed Yehuda in a choke hold, "To your throne? Indeed! To the throne I will send you. Make your way home, Jew!" With that Gaius slid the knife slowly from ear to ear, the blood gushing out in torrents. Yehuda's body fell limp. Wiping the blood from the sullied blade across Yehuda's slackened face, Gaius spit once more, then sauntered triumphantly away. He mounted his frightened horse, reclaiming his command and disappeared into the merchant's row.

Frantically pulling Yeshua behind him, Joses pointed at the crumpled body of Yehuda, bloodied and motionless. Collapsing, Joses cried, "We are too late! He lies dead. Oh, Yeshua!"

Yeshua forged forward, falling to his knees at his brother's lifeless form, and placed his hands on

Yehuda's face. Yeshua bellowed out to all reaches of creation, "No!"

Yehuda's eyes popped open into a blaze of light as if lightning had struck him. Just then a clap of thunder echoed from over the hills, in a sky without the sign of a cloud. Yeshua felt the flesh knit together, and with a gasp Yehuda reclaimed his breath. Yet, on his left side, the tissue under Yeshua's right hand remained puckered and raw. For a brief instant, the brother's eyes met and then Yehuda fell into a restorative sleep.

Cloven hooves, split tongues and entitled thoughts crowded Yeshua as the words from his mind leapt into the silence of time. Everything slowed as his mind rang out louder than ever he had known as he thundered his decree off the walls surrounding him, "Stop them!"

The horses reared, the masses engulfed the sentries, clamoring their leathered soles to scare the valiant steeds threatening to trample down their meager lives. They acted as if fear was not even an element of the equation in their mind, where it had easily been a mere second ago. All those who were in the square and surrounding alleys leapt to the soldiers, grabbing and pulling, shoving and shouting at them.

The words came with another clap of thunder from the cloudless sky. Even the eyes in the shadows and the slithers of temptation halted at the command repeated again from his lips, this time with much more emphasis, "Stop them!"

Joses' eyes were wider than Uncle Barabbas's amazement as he had watched clay birds flying in the skies all those years ago. Joses watched in astonishment as every member of the crowd, including

Uncle Barabbas and his cousins rushed toward their impending death beneath the hooves of the Roman soldiers. If they were to hinder a Roman division hell bent on carrying out whatever needed to be done… however, consequence was not even a thought in Yeshua's mind. Keeping them away from Yehuda was Yeshua's only desire.

As the hooves and screams escalated, Joses hand on Yeshua's arm snapped him back into the reality of the danger still threatening their lives. With a stronger desire for his safety, Joses cried to him from the alley where Yehuda lay, "Brother, let's go! We must go home. We will tell Abba about the rulings of the Roman Kings. Maybe we can find safety in the Southern kingdoms." But Yeshua did not move.

"Do not just stand there, Yeshua." Gathering up Yehuda in his arms, Joses kept speaking to the staggering Yeshua, spent from the outpouring of his soul and the severity of his actions. "Brother," Joses pleaded, "I wanted them to stop as well. But… I couldn't stop them…yet, you did! They all listened to you! As will everyone one day." Joses knew Yeshua's kingdom had already come with their birth, yet it seemed chaos reigned around every step his brothers made throughout the land.

"Yes, they will," Yeshua said trying to appease Joses' feverish bravado. "I have seen it in my dreams. Yes, now we must go!" Yeshua's dreams were vivid foreshadowing of the times to come. Joses had learned to trust the dreams of his eldest brother.

Yeshua fought the whispers in his mind. "I saw the hatred in your eyes!" teased the voice of the shadows that Yeshua usually was able to ignore. His weakened state could not drown it out as the horses and masses rushed by, making it seem as though a sand storm was passing through. He jeered at Yeshua, "You wanted them to stop as much as me! Yet you feared the power within. I see your eyes when the older boys used to push you. You wanted them gone then, as much as we did now!"

With the charisma like the snake charmers they had encountered in the east when they travelled with Uncle Yosef of Arimathea, Yeshua seemed to sing behind the words he knew would speak to some part of his mind, "Gone? No, not be gone, but perhaps simply to stop. Maybe there is another way. Perhaps they fight with us because of jealousy. That might be the only means of expressing their desire to have what we know is in our hearts and within our reach. Yet sometimes you are right, they do now and again get me quite angry! Though I do not fear the anger – it is what comes after the anger that brings me concern. That is what concerns me of you, my mirror."

As a true mirror, the voice recoiled, "What comes after the anger is the fulfillment of desire! They will stop as everyone moved to stop the Romans just now. I did that! However, it was not anger behind my words. Your perceptions of my thoughts are no more valid than how a Roman understands your ways." And then the voice broke out in maniacal laughter.

Not often paying attention to these wandering and sometimes nonsensical meanderings, Yeshua began to question his actions. Was it anger, or was it directed and determined desire that moved those people? He was truly not angry, merely deeply determined to show the strength of their people to those vile human beings from a far off land. Miriam knew of their gifts from the Lord, yet what could they really do with them?

In the years before the family went to live with the Essenes, Barabbas would look at them with awe and wonder, yet most of the time it seemed to be concern of what power resided behind their eyes. Their Uncle Barabbas was one of their favorites. He would run right along with them, even though he was as advanced in age as their mother. He could kick a stone farther than the hawk could climb on a clear day.

Yeshua remembered the fun they all would have by the shores of the creeks and rivers. Barabbas could make the finest of toys from the driest of soils if he had enough water. He would always spit on every clay thing he made. Sometimes he would also put a stone inside it. "Give it a heart, some love and a breath of your soul, boys. That is how they taught us to create life as the Lord created all of us. One day I will see to it that Yosef takes you to the Nazarene priests with all the scrolls to learn from. These Masters of education your parents have sought for you know nothing of the wise men in the hills. Angels dare not enter these cities, where the supposed Masters hovel in depravity."

As Yeshua regained his composure, the laughter faded. Then, from the deeper recesses of his mind, Yeshua heard Yehuda murmur, "He can be so condescending when he speaks the truth. You always know where to find peace. You always know the heart of love in even the darkest of recesses."

Hearing those thoughts, with those peaceful and still commanding amber eyes, Yeshua looked at his brother in the arms of Joses, "Let's go home."

Yehuda sighed as deep as the northern winds blow at night, his entire being relaxed into his younger brother's arms.

Joses was listening to the winds and had a strange and eerie look on his forehead. "I hope Barabbas and our cousins are alright," he half mentioned as they walked through the dust.

"Give it a heart, some love and a breath…" and suddenly it registered within Yeshua's waking consciousness as he stopped in his tracks. He grabbed Joses, nearly spinning him around with his unbalanced load, and beseeched him, "Wait, Barabbas? Not Uncle Barabbas! Surely he wasn't in the crowd!"

Yet, he was.

Had Yeshua sent him to his death?

# ~ Chapter 21~

# Jealousy

*"I, Thomas, an Israelite, judged it necessary to make known to our brethren among the Gentiles, the actions and miracles of Christ in his childhood..." ~ 2 Infancy 1:1*

It was known throughout every village that there were wicked things about. Righteous men were as virtuous as the depravity they committed while their robes hung in darkened cabinets. The common, good and devout were acting like rabid animals frothing at the mouth to quench their latest desires. Sick and vile beasts roamed the territory while honest lives were trampled , and some even lost to the winds. Evil was a thought in every man's mind, even the holiest of them. The temples were wrought in gold and lavishness rivaling the kings of ancient days, while the true worth of this society found their next meal just as foreign as the next beggar around the corner.

When we think of our next meal, where it comes from, how it gets to our table, do we think of the how and the why? We give grace where grace belongs, give thanks to those that merit it, and we would consume no more than our purses can burden. We have been taught that the true Law resides in the hearts of every man, woman and child in existence. Yet that Law is bent and broken for the needs and perceived desires of those that hold the pen. These days, the use of such a device is even as rare as the next meal. Shall the words of the

Creator of every part of being be deafened by the glaring inequities surrounding us these days?

From yet another direction there was a member of a growing class of poor that had been crowding around Yeshua and his band of zealots, "Can you spare some grace, kind sir?"

A beggar amidst beggars, begging to take what is rightfully mine? Barely able to carry the weight of his own heart and the chains wrapped around them marked every crevice and crease around his aging body. His eyes were as white as the highest clouds in the sky, yet he knew that Yeshua stood before him. He knew in his heart that it was a Holy Man he was asking to lift him up.

Yeshua was a kind and generous man. "Sure. Eat well and be well, my friend."

Yehuda was a kind but cautious man. Simon Peter was equally wary with how this generosity battled with the ability of their group to survive. Yehuda whispered to Peter, "He hands out one more piece of silver. We need that silver to keep us from the sun, to shelter us from the rain – if it ever rains again – and would it not be better to usher this man to a meal or a place to rest?"

Peter hesitated, knowing the lessons they had learned and shared with those that had an ear to listen, yet something in him responded, "Surely it would be better to lead a man to drink instead of giving him an empty cup."

Noticing the distance Yeshua had from the reality around them, "My brother just seems so preoccupied. It's like he doesn't even have time for these people that seek his gifts out so fervently."

Yehuda moved up closer to his brother, gently pulling his elbow his way to draw his attention, "Yeshua, we should stop here in this town for the night. We are all weary and need some rest. We have been walking for what seems days." It was like the weeks following the baptisms by the river – camping under an outcropping of rocks, seeking out the cool comfort of a darkened cave. So many sought their counsel and wished to share their homes with them. Word of their charity and healings had spread faster than the Romans had engrained themselves into their society.

Peter flanked Yeshua on his right, "Master, why not take these people up on their generosity and kindness? A flattened bedroll in the stables of these homes we pass would be better than the stone pillows of late."

Many of the disciples were once the students of Yohanan. The growing resentfulness amongst the men centered its attention on Yeshua's wife. Every man is entitled to making a family, yet it was felt among some who had left behind their families or forgone the life of a family for the life of spirituality, that there was something amiss. It did not help that Miryam was an alluring woman or that her wisdom nearly equaled the teachings of their former master. Her features, similar to his, were out of place from the rest of the women of Judea. Her auburn hair that flowed like the waves of a cascading waterfall and her eyes when they caught the rays of the sun made the leaves of the trees jealous. It was sometimes a thought in many of the men's minds that her walk and demeanor was not like the others, and some were even tested in their commandments of the Law when the moon caught a hint of either hair or eye.

Yehuda spoke more for those who had less of the familiarity with Yeshua than he did, "Even she who washes your feet with the finest of our oils could use a moment of rest."

"Indeed, if that is how we all feel, unless most of us wish to amble through onto the next destination. I am sure that the blisters on everyone's feet, brother, constantly remind us of our arduous ascent to the Temple. The road may be long and filled with temptation of many kinds, yet the charity of others is something we should always entertain."

"Very wise of you, brother." Yehuda tried to temper his sarcasm, yet now and then Yeshua pressed on the wrong nerve.

"Yehuda, what is it that you are proposing? I am not opposed to finding rest here in this gracious town, yet if we are to make it to the Temple by the next moon, we must press on past our physical discomforts now and then, as the ability allows." When the blade of sarcasm was turned on you, and even the blade of truth, it was often said that it was better delivered by someone you know and in plain sight. "Even though others of us are willing to continue, I still ask of you, Yehuda, why need we stop here? Yehuda, my eager brother, the strength of the spirit keeps us all going and belief always brings us through the wilderness."

"Indeed, Yeshua. Indeed." They had spent almost three years traveling this wilderness, and they were finally making their way through civilization again. Civilization has its good and bad, yet Yehuda mused, "Yet the good lining of a comfortable bed would do a lot of good for us right now."

"We know not a single beggar in the next village, yet Father had many a friend here. Perhaps they, out of remembrance of him and how we ate at their tables long ago, will entertain us. Maybe we can negotiate fair labor for our stay. I hear Salome was taken in to one of these homes. It has been some time since we last saw her." Yosef always knew that providence supplied what a righteous man needed. If Yehuda's guidance brought them this far and with the groaning heard in the minds of the ones near him, anyone with vision would know that it was time to rest, even for just a brief time.

Yeshua seemed to be acquiescing to a short respite in this town. "We can pay whatever they wish of us, and yes, it would be good to see our youngest sister again if she is indeed a resident."

Yeshua pulled Yehuda close to him and spoke only so they could hear each other, "Why are you always so concerned about the purse and never of the weight within it that you carry? If we are to stay here or move on, one less piece of silver will not make the load any the lighter. What we need will be provided. You are our trusted advisor of our wealth; you keep our silver and supplies well accounted. If we must stay, let us find our sister if you think we should rest for a bit here with these people."

"We were both taught the same thing Yeshua. One piece more, one piece less, yet no more the lighter. One less will no more be the way we go about this desert – one less mouth to feed, one less weight in 'my purse.' You know the weight of 'my purse.' Perhaps."

Often the discussion ended past the vocal exchange inside Yehuda's head. "He analyzed life beneath that tree for hours as a boy, while we fashioned other miracles for the richest in the land – only just enough to put food on the table. The words of accolade and desirousness fed his dreams beneath the olive trees. These people stare at us. Stares... I hate staring eyes."

Anger had always been a demon of Yehuda's, while calmness and serenity were Yeshua's publicized demons. Many ask themselves, calmness and serenity as demons? They were demons to the support of a family that loved Yeshua so much. As intelligent and profound as he had always been, Yehuda's brother marveled at each of their strengths of will and devotion to their family.

~~~

"Why cannot I go with you Father?" Yeshua would ask of Yosef. Miriam never wanted him in danger, yet often would both brothers wander into the town or explore Jerusalem during the holy days.

It was Yehuda who would lay awake at night while Yeshua was in the gardens, tinkering on the lowliest of field marble and shaping smooth the timber of the tumbling, drought-ridden weeds. "How does Father turn that stone into the work of an angel?" Yeshua would ask.

Just as Yosef had taught, Yehuda would reply "You just let it come out of the rock." The earth beneath our feet, the stones riddled throughout these hills all had stories to tell. Yosef would sit for hours with the largest of stones the Kings and Princes asked him to inlay. He would press his ear to them. Feel every curve of what seemed to be a precision cut block of the hardest marble. Yosef could count the host of heaven's angels on the head of a nail. While Yeshua would embrace the trees with Miriam, Yosef would have Yehuda feel every blade of grass surrounding their hands as they sat on the hillsides near their home in Galilee. Hours would go by looking at the skies for inspiration for their next masterpiece. Searching around for something to illustrate what to him was a simple idea, yet to someone so intuitively visual, Yehuda noticed one of Yosef's clouds floated by them, "See that cloud up there?"

Yeshua said puzzled, "Yes. What of it?" He could see a host of heavenly angels sitting on the sloping hills of Heaven just above their heads. "It shades our eyes from the glaring sun. It keeps you and our family cooler while you work, yet what am I looking to see?"

Yehuda shook his head, "Watch it. Wait for something to appear." As the Essene taught, if they quieted out the mind enough, they could have heard the choir beginning a testament to the Lord's majesty unfolding before their eyes.

"A bird, Brother, it's a bird! With a long beak, and a quirky little tuft of feathers off the back of his head."

His thoughts leapt from his mind, "He sees birds, while the rest of us see angels from the Lord." Placating Yeshua's imagination, he replied "Yes, indeed, a bird. What of that grouping over there?"

~~~

Sitting at the table of this kind landowner, the rest of them were enthralled in the stories and parables that Yeshua was sharing with their benefactor. They all found rest of the mind, body and spirit. It was the relief that Yehuda knew they all needed. He looked across the room at his brother and received the acknowledgment for which he was looking.

However, Yehuda seemed to be haunted. The discomfiting and evil eye of the dark ones staring from the shadows is what he developed an eye to see. They watched him, haunted him, and bade him to return to do their bidding in whatever game they were contriving.

Stares… he truly hated staring eyes. The simple times when they were simple boys, before they saw the darkness behind the shadows, were only a few years behind. In his mind, they were even closer.

# ~ Chapter 22 ~

# A Savior Reaches Out

*"But when the Pharisees heard this, they said, 'This man drives out demons only by Beelzebul, the ruler of the demons.'" ~ Matthew 12:24*

"Yehuda, we need to talk." He could hear Yeshua in his head so vibrantly; it was just like when they were kids. He had learned to shut Yeshua out over the years growing up, yet now he was as clear as the reflection of my face in the anger in Miryam's eyes. "We need to talk." Indeed they did.

Most would have seen the conversations with the darkness around him as mindless grief; Yehuda was alone in the corner talking to what seemed to be thin air. "We need to talk? That will be a phrase throughout time that will ring a sour note on everyone's ear. Sitting here in the corner of this room, knowing all who slumber have seen the last of you, I dare to ponder the idea of what I am about to hear. If you say it's time for me to sleep, I think I'll just run." The escape from Yeshua's words and his touch was the trick of escaping the command to rest, and yet Yeshua's touch was something of which he no longer yearned. His touch was truly more magical than Yehuda ever realized.

Knowing now there was no escaping his touch or his words now, "I'll just keep an eye on the little ones."

"There is no escaping fate, my brother." Now that everything that has been revealed, now that everything was done, now that His will had been met, now that he was left to carry such heaviness; it was time.

"The last time I heard, 'We need to talk,' I was in no place to listen."

"Indeed, you were not, Yehuda. Yet now you are."

~~~

Trapped in the darkest corner of his own making, Yehuda believed not a single soul in creation could find him here. Not even the numerous crawling six and eight-legged monsters even thought to call this desperate corner of existence a home. The wash water was tossed out a western window of a hovel further up the alley. As a rat dashed scurried past, "What was that, more persecutors chasing me? They surely know I crouch here in the darkness.

"Huddled here in this heap is perfect for the garbage that should have been cast to the fire long ago! All that follows me here still stares at me from the shadows. I so deeply hate it when people stare! Peering into shuttered windows, or some thing or someone, or at some place where you have not been invited – is the most supremely inappropriate and rudest thing humanity has chosen to evolve.

"You! In the alley!" came from some grimy doorway in the gloom of this night.

"The shouts from the alleys around here echo my impending capture. Surely this is the end, the bottom, the true sentence to the Sheol I deserve.

"The weight of my head upon this wall should bring it and the surrounding building to ruin, yet the cold stone brings such a sense of clarity. At least it brings calmness from the voices, from the tormentors, those precious demons in my head.

"I have become more a brother to the darkness, the wicked, the garbage, the casted filth; more to me a brother than the holy example in my memory."

Yehuda desperately yearned for his brother's touch. The simple placing of his hand on his shoulder at the right moment would calm the demonic hordes at the gate of his mind. Typically, that was all he needed to carry him out of the obscurity creeping around inside. Yet, after all they had been through! He looked back on the words he had chosen, the thoughts he had exchanged and the decisions he had made – the decisions made by both of them.

It had been what seemed years since he last saw Yeshua. He left him in tears in the doorway of the home he had made with Miryam. The children had been put to bed, and the torment in his mind was too much. He knew he had to leave his brother after all the years they had spent together. "If you will only think of yourself, Yehuda, then perhaps your self should be the one with whom you walk." Those words had echoed in his mind since he turned his back that evening. As he walked into the darkness that night, the last words he heard were, "I will find you when you need me! I will find you!"

The commotion on the streets was surely for this wretched creature. "Find him! He couldn't have gone too far!"

"Not too far indeed, I am right here! I am cowering in this cold corner, the heavy and hurried footsteps clamoring all around, echoing through every nook and cranny of the maze of streets and alleyways. I know I have lost the way!

As ironic as that now sounded inside, after stumbling over this cart and that basket, shoving away this person and that bystander, climbing over this and that, he knew something was happening.

The screams of the surprised women guarding their homes as he fervently broke through them trying to escape those chasing him still haunted him. "Those glaring devils, those evil and never ending persecutors!" They were always at his heels.

"I just saw him run through that house! He's over here!" The demons confounded their senses. The crowd stopped and then they hurried on. However, the rest of the demons Yehuda could see chasing him swarmed in and simply stared. They stared right through him, "Hide, trash, hide!" hissing vile accusations that stung like brands on his skin, penetrating to the skin of his soul.

The shriek of the wind chilled his bones. "Crouch down and look like the trash you are!"

The grading of the stones beneath him even chided him, "You should have been cast out in the beginning." Ghostly faces rushed through his body from all directions, dragging chains and barbs that slashed through him. The torments of the gouging lashes should have produced gaping wounds on his skin, and shreds of his garments, they felt so real. He screamed in agony and pain, "What do you want from me?"

He shouted again in the loudest voice he could muster, yet it trickled out with a faint whisper, "Leave me alone! Go!" If he had actually shouted as loud as he wanted, the others that were actually there to rescue him would hear his cries and save him from these demons.

"Do you want to infect the rest with your ranting and raving?" The demons that circled him chided one by one, "Devil! Devil! Devil!"

"Ranting and raving indeed!" Being chased by the taunts and teasing of those evil children. The ringing of their hecklings and sharpness of mockers shot through to the core of his soul. "What do you want?" He screamed with the embers of his shriveling body. Yehuda had not had anything to eat in days, possibly weeks. The dehydration was evident on his lips and eyes as if he had been walking in the wastelands for months.

In his mind he now could hear the singing like in the hills when he was young. He and Yeshua would often hear the sounds of angels rejoicing from the graceful knolls. As the singing grew louder, in this respite from the howls, he recognized the sounds as a sign, a call from the better part of him that he had stifled, yet now the part that came crashing through. He began to pray as he was taught; not just as a call out for assistance, yet more of an escape into the realm to speak directly to the one who had been in his head all the time these last few days yet was too ashamed to face.

"I have time and time again failed to keep your face from following my own. I don't deserve it! I long for your touch! You reach out to me with a simple placing of your hand on my shoulder." He began to pray out loud.

"Father, I cry out to you! Your presence is all around us. I feel it in every stone beneath my feet. I feel you ebbing and flowing through everything."

Perhaps the shouts and stares were his salvation. Yet the stares…the stares!

"Soften this hardened soil, and hallow a place for your seed of wisdom to grow. Your will sings clearly in my mind. Let this tree bear clean and sacred fruit once again!"

Seeing the ferns and flowers shine with the magic of their creation was a memory far too faint to hold in his hand again.

"Bring to me the knowledge and grace needed to bring forth the glorious fruit of your will. Untie the tangled threads of destiny which bind me, and release others from the entanglement of my past."

So much had those hands been calloused and cut, bruised and beaten with the misguided desires to have more. The desires to gather and horde had held him back for so long. The things he had done, justifying them for the greater good of the people. The evil placed upon all of them by the Romans and invading foreign kings and emperors. Surely the reckoning makes sense in some fashion. So many have seen the sharp end of his anger and had been cast away for some rationalization. Could they ever find forgiveness in their heart for such trash?

"Do not let me be seduced by that which would divert me from the true purpose, yet illuminate my heart and mind to the opportunities of the now. You, Lord, are the ground of the fruitful vision, the birthing-power, and the fulfillment, and all are gathered in the desire to be made whole once again. With this cry out to you am I seeking your repair, my Lord."

Are there enough binders, enough forgiveness in the hearts of all he had shamed, to mend this broken vessel?

"Send me a savior, Lord! Send me a lamp through the darkness and return my heart as it once was! Lend me a hand of your grace and mercy, and I will be an instrument of your will forever more."

He had reached the bottom of all that could be bleak and contemptible in his life. He so longed and yearned for that hand, the embrace, that forgiving and welcoming acceptance back to the family he had left behind in the darkened night.

"This I seal in love, faith and truth. Ahmeen!"

Surely the hand of grace and mercy would be able to lift him from that hole.

"This I seal in love, faith and truth. Ahmeen!"

No more would the blade and curses be the tools of his perceived righteousness.

"This I seal in love, faith and truth. Ahmeen!"

He just needed his brother in his life again. Yeshua always knew how to make the tribulations melt away and craft the world just as it should be. He would have an answer wrapped in a silent glance. That hand on his shoulder always spoke more to the glory of creation than any pardon he could be granted in this damned world.

"Yeshua, where are you? I need you, my mirror, my brother! Find me! Find me... find... me."

A hand, no more than a single breath away from asking for it, was softly placed on his shivering shoulder. That hand was so familiar and known to him from even before the beginning.

It had to be a trick! He shrank deeper in fear that they had finally caught him, and he doubted he could cower further into this block and mortar prison.

"Yehuda! Come out from that hole you have dug!"

Could it be? Could it be that his prayers had been heard from the depths of damnation?

"Come with me, dearest brother." The light of angels shined into the darkest corners of this alley Yehuda had claimed as his death bed. The warmth of his brother's hand on his right shoulder was the answer he believed would never come.

"Yehuda, we need to talk."

~~~

Yehuda was brought out of the nightmarish memories and his salvation by Yeshua only to be thrust into a present terror, "We need to talk about them. We must talk about..."

Yehuda interrupted him. He rarely got the upper hand in a conversation, let alone the ability to find a breath to speak his own mind. Now that they were inside his mind, this was the perfect opportunity to interject, "We definitely need to talk. We need to talk about them; the children who look at me and see their father with a scar in his beard hair and know that I am not you. I knew I will always be Uncle in their eyes, yet their eyes find a hint of their father in every glance thrown my way." Would the anguish of loss perpetually fester with their Uncle now set as their guardian?

When the memory found their gaze recognizing the scar, that wound would be the seal on their longing. "As much as I wish every day for this scar to be wholly gone, it reminds me of your touch, your grace. Yet, as the angel told us years ago, 'A wound caused by the blade of David, the same metal hewn in the fires of Creation as the sword of MichaEl, can never be wholly erased from the flesh of the earth.' Yet, I breathe when breath had finished with me. It was the only thing that kept me from your place. This scar will remind them always that I am not their father, yet no scar will keep them from my heart."

They were just as much his joy as they were Yeshua's.

~~~

Miryam, still at table, eyed them both. "She has been through so much. I dare not even fathom what she is going through in these darkened moments, Yehuda. If..."

"She is faced with raising all seven of the little ones and still longs for the sweet embrace and loving understanding of your hand. Now she fusses and fidgets not knowing if the dawn will illumine or set fire to all that we have tried to accomplish." Looking over at Miryam, with a hint of sarcasm dripping from the faint grin on his face, Yehuda continued after the awkward pause, "I beg you, please, let me stand in judgment instead." Returning to a more serious tone, "My life would be forfeit already if not for you."

Many silent moments passed then Yeshua agreed that his brother's last statement was true. With a sigh, he kissed Yehuda. The illusion of a scar now lingered on Yeshua's jaw in plain sight. Yehuda reached up to his own beard, but feeling the pucker, was disappointed. Yeshua held a polished plate to his brother's face, and to his amazement, no trace of that which distinguished him was evident to a searching eye.

The plan was brilliant! They would dress in similar robes and when Yehuda led the Sanhedrin to the appointed spot, the kiss would exchange their identities, just as it had moments ago. In the darkness of the grove, with their limited sight, they would take the unblemished lamb. Yeshua could escape with his wife and children while they arrested Yehuda instead.

~~~

How often is a man betrayed by the promise in a kiss? How often does one man forfeit his life to save his brother? How often could one man save the world from impending destruction?

# ~ Chapter 23 ~

# The Sunset

*"He gave them the cup in like manner, when the meal was over. 'This cup,' He said, 'is the new Covenant ratified by my blood which is to be poured out on your behalf.'" ~ Luke 22:20*

Miryam considered that the sense of loneliness is multiplied by being out at sea. She struggled with her thoughts: "There's nothing, no land, no shapes or forms that come between you and the setting sun. And yet that sun seems so far away. As if you could sail all night and never be any closer. Yet that is the way this ship sails, and this is the direction that all will travel. We are pointed to the west. The dawn will be at my back. May we rest in this darkness! May we be safe in the open sea to see the dawn once more!"

Near sunset on the first day on the trading vessel, Miryam stood silently at the prow. The salt spray had simply added a bit more moisture to her already sopping cheeks. Leaning against his mother, Miamon stood tall at the rail, his hair tossed about his unreadable face. Her gentle fingers swept the dark strands from his soulful eyes. Maimon's hair was the same texture as his father's with the flash of auburn that her side of the family carried. This last year had stripped Miryam of so much of her fiery passion and the proof was left shining in silver streaks. Without speaking, the two of them stood watching the sun sink lower into the

Mediterranean, while the waters reflected the deepening reds. With the rhythmic crashing of the waves, her mind drifted to the last time she had brushed her brother's hair from his leathery face.

~~~

His eye was bruised and his face so battered that he was nearly unrecognizable. Too weak to even swat the flies away from the crusted blood and his swollen eye, she wondered how long he would endure the filthy cell. The guards had allowed Miryam to enter without hesitation. There was no question of her identity and they were humbled by the man most had gone out to hear speak. Some had even emerged changed in the Jordan. Yet, they were simply under the order of the Herod that Yohanan had disgraced. Barely able to swallow from the cup she held to his cracked lips, he rebuked her for being in such a wretched place. As if they were still children, she ignored him, and instead smiled. She washed his face as gently as she could, and then dipped his hands in the basin. His hands were clean. Miryam stepped out as the young guard lifted his soiled robe from his emaciated body and poured the basin over him. Dressed in the fresh robe only seemed to emphasize how much he had suffered beyond the ravages of his own desert isolation. This place smelled of death and all here knew it. Not even the Jordan could wash this stink away.

"Miryam, can he do this?"

"Brother, do you love me?"

"How could you ask such a question?

"Because, my brother, when all is lost to us, when Mother died and our Father, we knew already what they had known. That a messenger of God was there to announce our becoming! We have seen more than most eyes shall ever see. More than most families will ever endure, and yet you, my brother, you forsook your own happiness to serve our Sovereign Lords! Once you knew what he was, once you witnessed my betrothal, a husband I was given but a brother I had lost. Did you not love me? Don't you think that he loves me as much? Do not ask if he can drink from the cup that was filled before we were born! The greater question, the question I ask myself, is can I bear one more day without drinking it up instead? Instead of watching and waiting for the Light to save us all?"

The Herods, Annas, Caiaphas, the disgrace, Yohanan's face, Yeshua's face, Barabbas. The horror, the pain, the seething hate that could not sway her brother or her husband or dear Barabbas no matter how much they tried to beat it into them! Would these be the images she would remember the most? No! No! Looking out to the sunset like the blood on the water – soon it would fall beyond the horizon. By grace these memories too would fade.

No wine had ever touched her brother's lips, and yet she had feasted and drank the finest vintage, greater than any vineyard. Sometimes, however, she drank more from his eyes than anything that had ever touched her lips. The last meal that they had shared was at table with all who loved him. Staring into the sunset, she thought if only she could dip her cup into the waters before her, she could gather enough. The blood red sea, the scarlet threads and the crimson flashed brighter than rubies, just as his blood was there everywhere in her mind.

She questioned: Did they all understand what he had been saying? Did they understand what he knew? That we would never sit with him, never laugh with him, that we would never be a family again? So many riddles were in his stories. So much allusion in his words! Every phrase she questioned in the twenty years she had been by his side.

At that last supper, he told us that he would betray one of us. But did he betray all of us, or had, in fact, our own desires betrayed us all? Peter denied him to save his own freedom, his own life, but isn't that what Yeshua wanted? Was it just an acknowledgement and not a warning?

He would never have allowed his brother to take his place because how could he live and not be who he always was? The switch would have been a lie and he would not sacrifice his brother and yet live. He had made his choice long before we ever knew there was a question.

Somehow I even believe he orchestrated the affairs so that his beloved Uncle Barabbas was freed to protect his mother and father. Who knows what an orphan can accomplish in his search to become closer to the Father that was lost to him! Justus has family now to protect from the envious sight of the Sanhedrin and the Romans.

It will be good to be far away and yet we do not leave the Romans behind – but our people, our own tribe, those we can escape! How peculiar it is that the Roman, Pilate, would not pass judgment, and that he washed his hands of his involvement. The guards, those awful men, we cannot blame for how they treated him! To them, he was just another foreigner - just another criminal was hung to die. But now their lives would never be the same. They had witnessed the Light for themselves.

~~~

Yehuda sat below deck as the calm waves lapped against the side of the boat. Exhausted from the trek to the shore, most of the children were lying on their mats fitfully dreaming. Yet, Yehuda could not rest. Just the memory of, "Sleep now," brought a thought that if he slept, life would change again. Enough change had occured for a while.

"Uncle, where is Mother?" asked Elisheva.

"She is above on the deck with Maimon. You should get your sleep." Yehuda and Elisheva had a rocky relationship, yet their stations allowed an understanding of which outranked the other.

The light from the hatch to the upper deck was beginning to darken, and in the darkness Yehuda felt there would be some solace. The voices were still somewhat silent, yet there was a voice he longed to hear again. The intrusions from the shadows had remained at bay since that horrid day.

What had happened? Was it a miracle designed by the Creator, or something else? Had it all been a dream? Oh, how he wished he could wake and see his brother again.

The light from above grew dimmer. The bleats of the animals at the end of the cargo area were signaling the end of their day. The shifting of some other freight in packing crates creaked and groaned, resettling with each sway in the waters. This would surely be a long journey.

Yehuda lit the lamp hanging beside him to cast a better view of the children. They were all restless, and rightly so – none of them foresaw any easy sleep in the near future.

The only light was the one by his side. All he had were the clothes on his back, some meager belongings in the chests of supplies, and his personals in his satchel. He reached down to unclasp the ties that kept it secure.

This satchel had been a treasure of Yosef's. One of the gifts his Abba had given him before leaving their homeland behind. It formerly carried his father's tools, and now it held memories. A bound book of blank pages to retain important memories, ink and stylus to engrave his thoughts upon the parchment, some medicinals he always carried, and three stained nails. He reached in without looking in the dim light and removed the wretched spikes.

He murmured louder than he knew, as Uzit watched him and heard him say, "Wretched pieces of iron," as they tumbled between his hands.

"Uncle, where did you get those? They look quite strong. A long fire surely forged them." Uzit had an affinity for metals and their forging. She was womanly yet strong and could hold her own against her older brother and cousins back home. Indeed, back home. Where would they call home now?

Yehuda's hands ran over every inch of the leather that bound together the parchment Yosef of Arimathea had given him. "Use this to remember the good times and chronicle the ones to come. Never forget, Yehuda, the reason you are here now. They are yours and you are theirs. He will always be watching for he has risen. Glory be to the long walk before you."

"Indeed, Uncle. I will always remember. That I know. Emblazoned forever in my heart and soul, I doubt any stories I write in here will equal the memories in my mind and body." His Uncle he would never see again. His Ima and Abba were under the watchful and loving dominion of Uncle Barabbas, now known as Justus. The stories he would tell the children when they wished to listen.

Yehuda looked upward through the decking and into the heavens, "What do I do, Yeshua? What do I do now?"

"Remember... Tell... Love..." These were the words he heard in his mind. They seemed so faint, yet still strong in his heart.

Remember? He would never forget.

Love? Surely many opportunities would arise to share the love in his heart.

Tell? Now, that would be the difficult one.
What would he tell?
Who would he tell?
Better yet...
Who would listen?

~~~

Miryam felt so weak, so fragile and frail standing there with their son, Maimon. She envied Yeshua of the strength he had to carry that timber. How could a body, how could a man, endure so much pain? Even shrugging off Veronica's healing salve. It is like he carried the pain of all of us to that hill. The sounds of the mallets striking metal and flesh and yet, he sacrificed all so that we might live.

    Turning to go below deck, toward the light of the family that awaited her, with Maimon by the hand, Miryam must only think of living now.

www.ingramcontent.com/pod-product-compliance
Lightning Source LLC
LaVergne TN
LVHW041622070426
835507LV00008B/397